SPAIN

WHAT EVERYONE NEEDS TO KNOW®

WILLIAM CHISLETT

OXFORD
UNIVERSITY PRESS

OXFORD
UNIVERSITY PRESS

Oxford University Press is a department of the University of Oxford.
It furthers the University's objective of excellence in research, scholarship,
and education by publishing worldwide.

Oxford New York
Auckland   Cape Town   Dar es Salaam   Hong Kong   Karachi
Kuala Lumpur   Madrid   Melbourne   Mexico City   Nairobi
New Delhi   Shanghai   Taipei   Toronto

With offices in
Argentina   Austria   Brazil   Chile   Czech Republic   France   Greece
Guatemala   Hungary   Italy   Japan   Poland   Portugal   Singapore
South Korea   Switzerland   Thailand   Turkey   Ukraine   Vietnam

Oxford is a registered trademark of Oxford University Press
in the UK and certain other countries.

Published in the United States of America by
Oxford University Press
198 Madison Avenue, New York, NY 10016

© Oxford University Press 2013

Library of Congress Cataloging-in-Publication Data
Chislett, William, 1951–
Spain : what everyone needs to know / William Chislett.
pages cm
Includes bibliographical references and index.
ISBN 978-0-19-993646-5 (pbk. : alk. paper)—ISBN 978-0-19-993644-1
(hardback : alk. paper)   1. Spain—History—20th century.
2. Spain—History–21st century.   3. Spain—Politics and government—
20th century.   4. Spain—Politics and government—21st century.
5. Spain—Economic conditions—20th century.   6. Spain—Economic
conditions—
21st century. I. Title.
DP272.C47 2013
946.08—dc23
2012051579

"What Everyone Needs to Know" is a registered trademark
of Oxford University Press.

5 7 9 5 6 4
Printed in Canada
on acid-free paper

SPAIN

WHAT EVERYONE NEEDS TO KNOW®

*For Sonia, Tomás, and Benjamin, without whom the opportunity
to write this book would never have arisen.*

Spain is not so different, so special as it is manipulatively said to be. We must stamp out once and for all the idea that Spain is an anomalous country ... a case apart, an exception that justifies any action.

—Julián Marías, philosopher
and sociologist (1914–2005)

Spain is different.

—Tourism slogan in the 1960s during
the Franco dictatorship

CONTENTS

2 The Franco Regime, 1939–1975   **42**

5 The Return of the Right, 1996–2004   131

6 The Socialists Strike Back, 2004–2011   154

LIST OF TABLES

ACKNOWLEDGMENTS

I thank Angela Chnapko, my editor at Oxford University Press, for encouraging me to write this work, and Katherine Ulrich for her meticulous copyediting. I am also grateful to the following people who over the years, and in different ways, have enhanced my understanding of Spain: Tom Burns, Salustiano del Campo, John Carlin, Guillermo de la Dehesa, Michael Eaude, Fernando Fernández, Soledad Fox, Ian Gibson, Ferdi Grafe, Mauro Guillén, Jorge Hay, José Antonio Herce, Gabriel Jackson, Michael Jacobs, Emilio Lamo de Espinosa, Elvira Lindo, Javier Marías, Mariano Morcate, Marcelino Oreja, Víctor Pérez-Díaz, Philip Petit, Paul Preston, Michael Reid, Gabriel Tortella, Giles Tremlett, Nigel Townson, and José Varela Ortega. Given the compressed nature of the series *What Everyone Needs to Know*, with much to be covered in a short space and the temptation to oversimplify a very complex country such as Spain, it was very important for me to have the manuscript read by a series of experts in different fields. I was very fortunate to persuade the following friends to read all or part of the manuscript, and I much appreciate the comments they made. The manuscript was read by: the historians Santos Juliá and Charles Powell, the novelist Antonio Muñoz Molina, the economist Valeriano Muñoz, the political scientist Diego Muro, the Oxford University academic Eric Southworth, and the author

Jeremy Treglown. Finally, Juan Manuel Cendoya, executive vice president, communications, corporate marketing and research, of Banco Santander, the euro zone's largest bank by market capitalization, and Alejandra Kindelan, global head of research and public policy of Banco Santander, arranged generous funding for some of my research, and with no strings attached. I thank them for their enlightened approach.

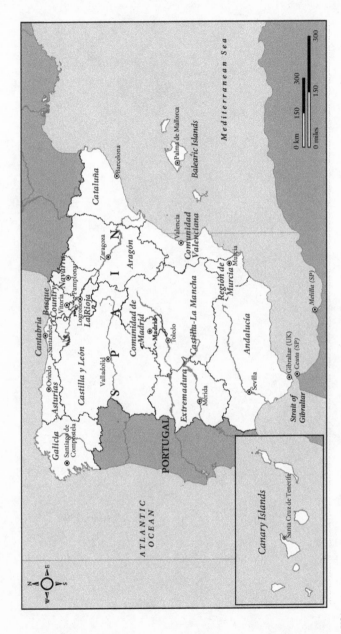

Alliance USA
Oxford University Press - Chislett/Spain
Map 1 - Spain
02/26/13 - Third Proof

SPAIN
WHAT EVERYONE NEEDS TO KNOW®

INTRODUCTION

I came to Spain as a young journalist in 1974, the year before General Franco, the country's dictator since winning the 1936–39 civil war, died. I had intended, after a short spell teaching English in Madrid, to return to journalism in Britain, but, instead, was swayed into staying by my then girlfriend (now wife) and Spanish friends. They were convinced the ailing ruler would not live much longer and post-Franco Spain would be a much more exciting place for a budding journalist than my home country.

According to a long-running joke at the time, thousands of Spaniards had short index fingers because every year they had tapped surfaces with it while saying that this really was the year when Franco would die. When he died in 1975 at the age of 82, Spain, a backwater known for little else apart from its mass tourism (today, Spain receives more than 57 million tourists a year, one of the largest numbers in the world), bullfighting, flamenco, siestas, and Europe's longest-serving dictator,[1] became overnight a major international story amid fears, played up not only by the more sensationalist international media, that the country would be plunged into another civil war.

I returned to journalism after Harry Debelius, the longtime Madrid correspondent of *The Times* of London, hired me to work with him. It was an intense three years during which

I interviewed many of the key protagonists of the transition to democracy, including King Juan Carlos, Franco's successor as head of state. The king, nicknamed Juan Carlos the Brief by Communists when he assumed the throne, as they predicted he would be swept away along with other remnants of the Franco regime, appreciated a joke against himself when we met. "Why was I crowned in a submarine? Because deep down I am not so stupid." Nothing could be truer, given the remarkably smooth transition to democracy (the first successful effort in Spain's turbulent history), which became something of a model for Latin American and former Communist countries. At the other end of the spectrum, I interviewed (in the sanctuary of the Biarritz golf club in southwestern France) José Miguel Beñaran Ordeñana (nom de guerre, Argala), a member of the violent Basque separatist ETA commando that detonated a bomb in December 1973 under the car of the 70-year-old Admiral Luis Carrero Blanco, the prime minister and Franco's political heir. The bomb hurtled Carrero Blanco's car into the air and over the roof of the San Francisco de Borja Church, where he had just been attending mass. Argala was later murdered in Anglet, France, near the border with Spain, by extreme-right-wing activists in similar circumstances.

In 1978, I moved to Mexico for the *Financial Times*. Such was the pull of Spain that after six years there and two in London at the FT's head office I left full-time journalism and returned with my family to Madrid for good. In 1976 my wife and I had bought a ruin of a cottage in a primitive village in Castile–La Mancha, the region where the novel *Don Quixote* by Miguel de Cervantes takes place. The village had no running water, largely unpaved streets, and a run-down primary school. Making a phone call involved going through an operator who was the daughter of one of the bar owners, and the nearest place to buy a newspaper was 17 kilometers away. For many years now, we have had running water, all the streets are paved, there is an automatic telephone exchange, Internet, a modern primary school, and a health center, and the local bakery sells newspapers. In the distance, on a hill overlooking the village's big reservoir, 25 100-meter-high wind turbines that look like a modern version of the giant windmills Don Quixote tilted at in a famous scene of the novel generate electricity. Today, Spain is the world's second-biggest producer of wind energy after Germany.

Spain has been transformed in many ways. Yet it is surprising how little is known about the country still (the euro zone's fourth-largest economy and the world's 13th) other than its stereotyped images, which persist and are out of sync with reality. When I first came to Spain, a colleague twice my age in London asked me whether Spain produced vehicles. At that time I knew next to nothing about the country, but I did know that it manufactured vehicles (more than 700,000, making it the world's ninth-largest producer). Almost 30 years later, in 2003, Spain was producing almost two million cars and was the eighth-largest manufacturer (in 2012, it was twelfth, with 1.9 million). José María Aznar, the then prime minister, visited the ranch in Texas of President George W. Bush and before seeing Bush chatted with one of his close advisors. The conversation went as follows: "And what is the chief product exported by Spain?" "Cars," replied Aznar. "No, I am asking about the number one product that Spain exports." "Cars," repeated Aznar. "No, no, what I want to know is which Spanish product sells most successfully abroad." "Yes, cars, cars," repeated an exasperated Aznar.[2]

The perception of Spain has changed little since then. How many people, for example, know that over the last 10 years many Britons now phone, switch on a light, bank, travel by the Tube (underground railway), fly out of an airport, including Heathrow, turn on a tap, or flush the toilet courtesy of several Spanish companies that have spent more than $75 billion buying companies in the United Kingdom? Or that Banco Santander, the euro zone's largest bank by market capitalization, has the largest banking franchise in Latin America and earns a much larger slice of its profits in

Brazil (it operates in many other of the region's countries) than in Spain? More than 20 Spanish multinationals occupy leading positions in the global market.

Moral attitudes have also undergone a radical change. My wife and I were barred from staying in a hotel in Ávila in 1974 because we did not have a *libro de familia* that proved that we were married. In fact we were, and no amount of protestations that this document did not exist for British couples made any difference. Moreover, we had been married in the registry office in Gibraltar, the UK overseas territory at the southern tip of Spain long claimed by Madrid, and at a time when the border with Spain was closed (by Franco in 1969). We were married there because during the Franco regime Catholicism was the state religion and it was difficult for a Catholic (my wife) to marry a Protestant. Civil marriages did not exist. The only way to get to the Rock, as it is called, from Madrid was by train to the port of Algeciras and from there to Tangiers by boat and then in another ship, an arduous journey. As the British novelist L. P. Hartley said: "The past is a foreign country; they do things differently there." This is certainly the case of Spain over the past 40 years.

Today, Spain is a non-confessional state and the Catholic Church has lost a lot of its power and influence, the border between Spain and Gibraltar is open (since 1982), and in the sphere of morals Spain is as liberal, if not more permissive, as other European countries. In 2005, Spain became the fourth country in the world to legalize same-sex marriage, after the Netherlands, Belgium, and Canada.

This book progresses chronologically, beginning in 711 with the arrival of Moors from North Africa, who ushered in Muslim rule in parts of Spain until 1492, and ending with the deep economic crisis. This approach enables readers to appreciate better Spain's progress over the centuries (sometimes one step forward and two steps backward) and understand more fully those aspects of its history that help to explain political tensions or conflicts that are of relevance today, especially concerning regional nationalism and state decentralization, and the religious cleavage. I have tried to make the answers to the questions in this book as watertight as possible, within the constraints of the series. This means that some duplication is unavoidable, as it is impossible to answer some of the questions without making references to material that appears in other answers. Place-names have been anglicized.

Spain has laid to rest many but not all the ghosts of its recent authoritarian past. Its democracy is vibrant, although the political class has lost the sheen it enjoyed during the 1975–1978 transition when consensus was the watchword and the guiding spirit. The widespread discontent with all parties, particularly the two largest ones, the conservative Popular Party and the Socialists, which between them have ruled Spain since the end of 1982, and with many of the state's institutions, stems to a large extent from the five-year recession. This recession was sparked by the bursting of an immense property bubble in 2008 after a more than decade-long economic boom. The spectacular collapse of the real estate and construction sectors was the main cause of Spain's rocketing unemployment rate to 26 percent in 2013, more than double the European average, and shook the country's economic, political, institutional, and social foundations. Much of the property bonanza, during which corruption flourished, was financed by regionally based savings banks with boards dominated by politicians and local businessmen rather than bankers. Many of these banks were saved from collapse by being nationalized.

The myopic political class, increasingly perceived as a caste, was widely blamed for an unsustainable economic model excessively based on bricks and mortar and far too little on knowledge, and for not using the boom to engineer structural reforms. Spain paid a high price for putting far too many eggs into one basket.

1

HISTORICAL BACKGROUND, 711–1939

What was the legacy of the Muslim presence between 711 and 1492?

Moors (Berber tribes) crossed over from North Africa in 711 and landed at a limestone mass they called *jabal-tariq* (Tariq's rock), or Gibraltar as it is known today. In just a few years they subdued the Visigoths, who had replaced the Romans (218 BC–AD 400) as the rulers of Hispania (the Roman name for the Iberian peninsula), and controlled most of what is today Spain and Portugal. (They got as far as Poitiers, France, where they were defeated by Charles Martel in 732 at the Battle of Tours). The Moors called the territory they occupied al-Andalus, and it was part of the caliphate of Damascus. The Islamic state was divided into five administrative areas roughly corresponding to Andalusia, Galicia and Portugal, Castile and León, Aragón and Catalonia, and Septimania (the area in France that today comprises Béziers, Carcassonne, and Narbonne).

The Christian resistance to the Muslims was initially concentrated in the mountainous region of Asturias in the north, where, in 722, Pelayo led the first significant victory over the Moors at Covadonga and began the 770-year drive to expel them from Iberia, known as the *reconquista* (Christian reconquest), a kind of crusade. There is a monument to Pelayo at Covadonga and a popular shrine to the Virgin Mary (Our Lady of Covadonga) in a cave. The heir to the Spanish throne, Prince Felipe (born in 1968), is known as the Prince of Asturias, in recognition of the region's importance as the cradle of Christian Spain.

The caliphate of Córdoba in southern Spain in what is today Andalusia ruled al-Andalus and part of North Africa from 921 to 1031, when it fractured into a number of independent *taifa* kingdoms (Granada, for example) as a result of infighting. Córdoba's Great Mosque, built on the site of St. Vincent's Church, which, in turn, rests upon the foundations of a Roman temple, became the second most important place of Muslim worship after Mecca. Today, it is one of the most visited sites in Spain. The other imposing Moorish building is the Alhambra palace in Granada. Arabic historians at the time called Córdoba the "jewel of the world." It was the largest city in Western Europe, with a population of up to 500,000 and magnificent palaces, gardens, fountains, and libraries, as well as a center of learning and translation at a time when the rest of medieval Europe was much less enlightened. Muslims were also tolerant of Christians and Jews; this coexistence of the three religions, though not always peaceful and harmonious, was relatively unique during the Middle Ages in Europe. The Muslims allowed the practice of other faiths provided the people holding them submitted to their rule and paid taxes.

The Muslims were also advanced in commerce, agriculture, and urbanization (they created new towns such as Badajoz and Almería). They capitalized on the Roman system of irrigation (Hispania was the breadbasket of the Roman Empire) and introduced new crops such as oranges, lemons, cotton, sugarcane, and rice. The enormous Roman aqueduct at Segovia is today a World Heritage Site, while the Tribunal de las Aguas (Water Court) in Valencia, established during the Muslim rule, still meets once a week to resolve irrigation disputes. Córdoba was renowned for its leather and metalwork (copper came from mines at Río Tinto), silk, weaving, and other skilled trades. Mercury came from Almadén. The Arabic influence was also significant on the Spanish language—for example, in words beginning with "al" like *alcalde* (mayor) and *alfombra* (carpet). Even the place-name Madrid, which did not become the capital of Spain until 1561, is of Arabic origin (it refers to a subterranean water conduit). The Muslim philosopher Averroës (1126–1198) lived in Córdoba and left his mark on European culture; it was mainly through him that the knowledge of Aristotle spread through Europe.

The Christians began to assert themselves, and by the early 10th century, there were kingdoms in León (later expanded and called Castile), Navarra, and the county of Barcelona, all of them ruled by warrior chieftains with striking names such as Sancho the Fat and Wilfred the Hairy. The Christian kingdoms occupied around 160,000 square kilometers in the year 1000 and had a population of 500,000, while the Muslim-held areas (known as *taifas*) covered 400,000 square kilometers and had a population of three million. The church (later cathedral) at Santiago de Compostela, the capital of Galicia in the northwest, has the shrine to Santiago Matamoros, St. James the Moor Slayer, who, according to legend, appeared as a warrior on a white horse at the battle of Clavijo and helped the Christians win against the vastly superior forces of the Moors. He is Spain's patron saint. Santiago de Compostela became the main pilgrimage center for Western Christianity; to this day thousands of people walk the route known as *El Camino de Santiago* (The Way of St. James). Given there are around one million Muslims in Spain today, mostly immigrants from North Africa, the title of Moor Slayer is rarely used for the saint for reasons of political correctness (see "How did Spain cope with the influx of immigrants"? in chapter 5). In 1085, Toledo, not far from the center of Spain, was captured, hugely boosting Christian morale. Toledo's importance in the history of the reconquista is epitomized by the Primacy of the Archdiocese of Toledo, so called because it had precedence over the other episcopal sees in Catholic Spain in the medieval and early modern era. Even today, the archbishop of Toledo is also known as the Primate of Spain, and he is often raised to the rank of cardinal by the pope. The most exalted warrior, and a national hero, was Rodrigo Díaz de Vivar (1043–1099), better known as El Cid Campeador. This name comes from the Arabic word *seyyid*, or lord, and *campeador* from the Latin *campi ductor*, or champion. El Cid, celebrated in "The Poem of Cid," believed to have been written by a 12th-century Spanish monk, was a kind of mercenary as he fought in the service of the Moors. He is best remembered as the central figure in the Christian conquest of Valencia. Other Muslim areas gradually fell to Christian forces; by 1264 the only one left was the kingdom of Granada, which was conquered in 1492. This opened the way to forge a more united country.

How did Ferdinand and Isabella forge a united Spanish kingdom?

The first steps toward a united Spain, albeit loosely articulated, came about as the result of the marriage, in 1469, between Queen Isabella I of Castile (1474–1504) and King Ferdinand II of Aragón (1479–1516). At the time, Castile was the largest and most populous kingdom, having some five million people. This dynastic union, the first in a series of composite monarchies based on the *aeque principali* approach which lasted until the early 18th century, was known as *los Reyes Católicos* (the Catholic monarchs). This approach involved separate administrative and taxation arrangements for each territory, but it also crystallized in many common projects and institutions (for example, Columbus's voyages of discovery). After winning the civil war caused by rival claims to the throne of Castile, the monarchs set up the Inquisition in 1478 to forge religious unity. Christianity was the driving force. Political unity, however, did not come to Spain until the 18th century, and then it was imposed by a different dynasty, the Bourbons. Aragon, for example, retained its Cortes (parliament), coinage, laws, and land tenure system, while Navarre's traditional laws, institutions, and customs saw no major changes until well into the

19th century. The spirit of the relationship between the territories and the monarchy was reflected in the oath of allegiance attributed to the Aragonese nobility. "We, who are each as good as you, and, all together greater than you, swear to accept you as our sovereign lord, provided you observe and cause to be observed, all our liberties and laws—but if not, not."

The badge of Isabella and Ferdinand and of subsequent Catholic monarchs was a yoke and a bundle of arrows. The yoke (*yugo* in Spanish) belonged to Ysabella and the arrows (*flechas* in Spanish) to Ferdinand. In the 1930s this badge became the symbol of the fascist Falange, which developed into the National Movement, the only legal political organization during the dictatorship of General Franco (1939–1975), and it can still be seen on the façade of some churches.

The original victims of the Inquisition, which lasted until 1820, were the *marranos* or *conversos*, Jews who had converted to the Christian faith and were suspected of secret adherence to Judaism. Tomás de Torquemada, the Grand Inquisitor, had urged Ferdinand in 1480 to expel all Jews from Andalusia, where most of them lived. This happened before the capture of Granada, the last Moorish kingdom, in January 1492, when all Jews (their number was estimated at no fewer than 150,000) were ordered to leave Spain, on pain of death. Their departure deprived Spain of a substantial part of its industrial, financial, and intellectual life.

Cardinal Francisco Jiménez de Cisneros, another Grand Inquisitor, clamped down on Muslims in 1499 when he publicly burned all the Arabic religious books he could find. In 1502, a royal decree ordered Muslims to either be baptized or go into exile. The majority stayed in Spain and became known as *moriscos*, or converted Moors. Spain thus became wholly Catholic, at least nominally, and gained a reputation for intolerance and cruelty that was to stick with it for many centuries. This gave rise to the *leyenda negra* (Black Legend), a phenomenon defined by the philosopher Julián Marías (1914–1995) as consisting of "the blanket disqualification of a country, founded on a few negative facts—and it does not matter a great deal whether they are true or false."[1]

Even though these Muslims were of pure or almost pure Spanish blood, as a result of centuries of intermarriage, and had converted, they continued to be persecuted as they were regarded as heretical Spaniards; they were expressly forbidden from taking baths, for example, as bathing was considered prima facie evidence of apostasy. The records of the Inquisition constantly refer to phrases such as "the accused was known to take baths.... "

The Protestant Reformation, triggered by the German monk Martin Luther in 1517 with his Ninety-five Theses, hardly penetrated Spain.[2] Successive monarchs energetically rejected it because it questioned the Catholic faith and their sacred role as defenders of the Blessed Sacrament. The status quo could not allow this because the creation of Spain as a nation came about as a result of the reconquest. If Charles I (known as Charles V, Holy Roman Emperor, between 1519 and 1556) had been king of just Spain, the Reformation would not have been much of a serious threat, but as emperor he could not afford religious divisions in his empire, as they would have had repercussions on Spain.

How did the Spanish Empire arise?

The year 1492 was a transcendental one for Spain and for the world. That year, Christopher Columbus set sail from Spain and on October 12, after 32 days at sea, landed on an island in the Caribbean he called San Salvador, which most scholars locate in the Bahamas. Over the next few years Columbus made three more voyages of discovery to America (the New World), opening the European colonial era and ushering in globalization.[3] This was a critical juncture in world history. His accounts of indigenous populations and animals never seen before by Western eyes encouraged many other explorers to brave the Atlantic in pursuit of wealth and fame, as well as Catholic priests with missionary zeal. Columbus's first voyage coincided with the publication of Antonio de Nebrija's Castilian Grammar, the first grammar book of any modern European language. It marked the clear supremacy of Castile over the rest of Spain. When Queen Isabella asked Nebrija what it was for, he replied: "Language, your majesty, is the companion of empire." The conquistadors imposed the Spanish language and Christianity on vast territories and populations that far exceeded those of Spain. The Catholic Church encouraged missionaries to learn indigenous languages so that they could use them to Christianize the population. One of the first books printed in Latin America was a Nahuatl grammar.

Dynastic marriages greatly aided the creation of the empire, particularly that, in 1496, of Philip, the son of Maximilian I, the Habsburg ruler of Germany (1486–1519) and Holy Roman Emperor (1493–1519), to Juana, daughter of Ferdinand and Isabella. Their son, the future emperor Charles V, succeeded Maximilian as Holy Roman Emperor, as Philip I died at the age of 28, and ruled both the Holy Roman Empire and, as Charles I, the Spanish Empire. Other factors in Spain's empire building were the relatively modest ambitions of potential rivals, the role of bullion in bolstering royal credit, and the collaborative disposition of the aristocracy who accepted, unlike their counterparts in France and England, that service to the crown defined nobility.

Spain was the preeminent and first truly global power during the 16th and most of the 17th centuries. It controlled most of what is today Latin America (with the main exception of Brazil, which was part of the Portuguese empire), parts of the United States, the East Indies (including the Philippines), and various European territories, including the Low Countries (the modern countries of Belgium, the Netherlands, and Luxembourg), the greater part of Italy, and some parts of modern France and Germany. It also established naval ascendancy in the Atlantic and Pacific and most of the Mediterranean. In 1571, Spain was part of the Holy League of Catholic maritime states that defeated the Ottoman Turks at the battle of

Lepanto (present-day Nafpaktos) in the Corinthian Gulf, dealing a severe blow to Muslim expansionism, the main threat to Western Christianity. There are many pictorial allegories of this battle, including Titian's *Allegory of the Battle of Lepanto*, hanging in the Prado museum in Madrid.

Spain gave up its European possessions after the War of the Spanish Succession (1701–1714), which several European powers fought over the unification of the kingdoms of Spain and France under the Bourbon monarch, Philip V. Latin American countries gradually gained independence during the early part of the 19th century and Spain lost the remnants of the empire—Cuba, Puerto Rico, and the Philippines—as a result of the Spanish-American War in 1898. In the last 20 years or so, a new kind of conquistador has emerged: Spanish multinationals have conquered significant parts of the Latin American economy (see "Why and how did Spain create multinational companies"? in chapter 5).

Who was Christopher Columbus?

Christopher Columbus (1451–1506) was born in or near Genoa. He moved to Lisbon around 1476 and, after failing to persuade King João II to finance an Atlantic crossing, transferred his quest for patronage to Spain, where King Ferdinand and Queen Isabella gave him a contract to discover the sea route to Asia. On August 3, 1492, he sailed with a fleet of three ships and 120 men from Palos in southwestern Spain. After stopping for final provisions in the Canary Islands, they sailed for more than a month without sighting land. Finally, on October 12, in Columbus's words, "something like a white sand cliff gleaming in the moonlight" appeared. This was a small island in the Caribbean. The date is commemorated every year throughout the Hispanic world. It is called El Día de la Hispanidad (Hispanity Day) in Spain and various names in other countries, including Columbus Day in the United States and Día de la Raza or Day of the Race, in Mexico.

Columbus claimed he had reached India; when he returned to the royal court in Spain in 1493, after his first voyage, he took six natives whom he called *indios* (Indians). He made three other trips, over which he discovered Cuba (although he believed he was in the fabled kingdom of Kublai Khan) and Puerto Rico, in which he founded the city of Santo Domingo on the island of Hispaniola (Haiti/Dominican Republic), and explored the coast of the American mainland. He recorded in his log in August 1498 that he had found "a very great continent, which until today has been unknown." Columbus fell out of favor with the crown and colonial administrators over the way in which he and his two brothers governed Hispaniola, including claims of torture. They were shipped back to Spain in 1500 in chains, accused of gross mismanagement. He spent six weeks in prison until King Ferdinand ordered his release and agreed to fund his fourth and last voyage. After his death, Columbus's body traveled as much as he did during his life. Results of DNA tests in 2004 suggested that he was not buried in Seville's Santa María cathedral but somewhere in the "new world," possibly the Dominican Republic.

Who were the conquistadors?

Among the first and best-known conquistadors were Hernán Cortés, who, with no more than 1,500 Spaniards, conquered the Aztec empire in Mexico in 1521, and Francisco Pizarro, who defeated the Incas in Peru in 1533. The Spanish forces were far outnumbered, but this was more than compensated by their horses, dogs, swords, and cannons, none of which the indigenous populations had seen. This stranger-effect was important. The Spaniards also took advantage of the civil discontent and intercommunal hostility in the Aztec and Inca empires, which made the indigenous population well-disposed to cooperate. Virtually all front-line fighting was done by native allies. Natives also became interpreters, the best known of whom was La Malinche, a Nahua woman and mistress of Cortés who gave birth to his first son, Martín. He is considered one of the first mestizos (offspring of European and indigenous American ancestry).

The Spaniards set themselves up as the new elite by taking control of the systems of taxation and forced labor that were already in place. They benefited too from being immune to the diseases they introduced, particularly smallpox, which killed hundreds of thousands of natives. Given the overwhelming odds against them, it is not surprising the Spaniards were amazed by the ease of their conquests and attributed them to a God-ordained mission and what they believed was their superior morale. There were reports of apparitions on battlefields of the Virgin Mary and St. James, Spain's patron saint.

The typical conquistador was in his late twenties, a fervent Catholic, not very literate, and mainly from what is today the region of Extremadura in southwestern Spain. They were not soldiers in the armies of the king. Conquistadors (men much more than women) tended to make the perilous crossing of the Atlantic of their own will and at their own cost, spurred by the prospect of gaining wealth and social status. The common image of the conquistadors is a bloodthirsty one. In fact, they were no more violent than the forgers of other empires. Lope de Aguirre, known as *El Loco* (the madman, brilliantly portrayed by Klaus Kinski in Werner Herzog's 1972 film *The Wrath of God*), was an extreme example of the brutality. His expedition in 1560 down the Amazon River was an orgy of violence. He was executed a year later for defying the Spanish crown and cut into quarters, which were sent to various cities across what is today Venezuela. Most of the conquered territories were peacefully gained as natives acquiesced without resistance. The Dominican friar Bartolomé de las Casas denounced the treatment of the natives in his *Short Account of the Destruction of the Indies*. He is seen as one of the first advocates for universal human rights.

What was the Spanish Golden Age?

Spain was at the height of its global power during the 1516–1556 reign of Charles I (known as Charles V, Holy Roman Emperor, between 1519 and 1556) and the 1556–1598 rule of his son Philip II. During this time it also experienced a flowering of literature and fine arts, known as the Siglo de Oro (the Golden Century)— although the period lasted more than 100 years. Miguel de Cervantes (1547–1616), author of *Don Quixote*, Fernando de Rojas (1465–1541), author of *Celestina*, the dramatists and poets Lope de Vega (1562–1635) and Pedro Calderón de la Barca (1600–1681), the painters El Greco (1541–1614), Diego Velázquez (1599–1660), and Bartolomé Esteban Murillo (1618–1682), and the composer Francisco de Vitoria (1492–1546), among the most well-known artists of the time, brought another kind of glory to Spain. The sharp contrasts between imperial grandeur and gradual decline at home can be read into *Don Quixote*. Like Cervantes's hero, Spain's elite had lost touch with reality.

Why did Spain go into decline in the 17th century?

The wealth that poured into Spain from trade with the colonies was monopolized by the monarchy. This money encouraged the Habsburg line of monarchs, from Philip I, whose reign was brief (1504–1506), to Charles II (1665–1700), to pursue their imperial ambitions closer to home and become entangled in futile and expensive European wars, notably the interminable Dutch War of Independence (1568–1648). The war began as a revolt in the Seventeen Provinces against Philip II (1556–1598), the sovereign of the Habsburg Netherlands, and ended 80 years later with the independence of the Netherlands. Philip ruled from the magnificent monastery and palace he had built at El Escorial near Madrid, which today is a UNESCO World Heritage Site. The floor plan of the vast building is in the form of a gridiron, chosen, according to traditional belief, in honor of St. Lawrence, who was martyred by being roasted to death on a grill. The crown's finances were in a bad shape. "Everything comes down to one thing: money and more money," lamented Philip. Foreign creditors, dazzled by what they assumed was endless wealth from Spain's colonies, provided loans to the nation. In 1588, the Spanish Armada set sail for England with the aim of overthrowing Queen Elizabeth I and ending English involvement in the Netherlands, as well as privateering—by figures such as Francis Drake (1540–1596), known as *El Pirata Draque*—against Spanish vessels returning home from the colonies laden with cargo. The smaller English vessels were more agile than the much larger Spanish ships; about 50 of the 130 ships from the so-called Invincible Armada failed to make it back home. The Spanish coffers were also eroded by the Thirty Years War (1618–1648), which was essentially a conflict between Protestants and Catholics in the Holy Roman Empire and Bourbon-Habsburg rivalry for preeminence. It was mainly fought in what is today Germany.

The wealth lulled Spain into a false sense of financial security. According to Martín González de Cellorigo, a 17th-century economist: "Our Spain has looked so much to the Indies trade that its inhabitants have neglected the affairs of these realms...wherefore Spain from its great wealth has attained poverty." Too much of this wealth was spent on building churches, palaces, and monasteries (more than 9,000 of these existed in 1626) and not enough was invested in human capital. Something similar happened during the delirium of Spain's 1994–2007 real estate boom, which, when the bubble burst, left more than one million unsold homes (see "What was the impact of the collapse of the property and construction sectors?" in chapter 6). Spaniards preferred unproductive professions in the church, the military, and the government, as they looked down on manual labor, industry, and commerce.

Another factor was religious intolerance, which stunted intellectual and scientific development. The Jews had been extensively involved in commerce and industry until they were expelled en masse in 1492, as were the Muslims in agriculture until they were forced into exile or to convert to the

Christian faith (those who did were known as *moriscos*) as of 1502. Between 1609 and 1614, some 300,000 *moriscos* were expelled from Spain, further depriving the agricultural sector, which was weak anyway because of the low fertility of soil and lack of expertise. As a result, Spain started to import wheat to feed its declining population. After growing strongly in the 16th century, Spain's population declined in the 17th because of outbreaks of plague and the expulsion of the *moriscos*.

Inflation was another factor that weakened the economy. The influx of gold and silver, particularly after the discovery of mines in Mexico and Bolivia, pushed up prices: too many people with too much money chased too few goods. Philip IV (1605–1665) inherited an empty treasury when he ascended the throne at the age of 16. His prime minister, Gaspar de Guzmán, the Count-Duke Olivares between 1621 and 1643, increased taxation in order to keep on financing involvement in wars, triggering revolts in Catalonia and Portugal (which was part of a dynastic union with Spain between 1580 and 1640). Philip put his finger on the problem when he said in 1626: "With as many kingdoms as have been linked to this crown, it is impossible to be without war in some areas, either to defend what we have acquired or to repulse my enemies." By then bronze *cuartos* were used in Spain more than silver *reales*, and over the next two decades silver coinage disappeared (it went abroad to pay for imports). In 1640 copper coins were recalled and stamped with double the value. Prices soared and sapped what commercial initiative existed. As if symbolizing the weakness of the Spanish state, Philip's son Charles II, the last Hapsburg, was so physically and mentally feeble (the result of too much royal intermarriage) that he was presented to court held up by strings as if he were a puppet.

What did the Bourbon kings contribute to the modernization of Spain between 1700 and 1823?

The Bourbons came to the throne in 1700 after Charles II died childless and left the throne vacant with two rival claimants.

as happened in 1936. The widespread use of these to achieve institutional change (there were more than 50 *pronunciamientos*, coups, plots, and military mutinies between 1815 and 1936) underscored the weakness of civil society.

Moderate and Progressive governments were both led at times by generals: the former by Ramón María Narváez and Leopoldo O'Donnell (of the Liberal Unionists) and the latter by Baldomero Espartero and Juan Prim. In 1868, Prim, an admirer of Abraham Lincoln, "pronounced" for a "Spain with honor," forcing Isabella to flee to France.

The so-called Glorious Revolution (*La Gloriosa*) ushered in a new constitution, which held out the prospect of a more representative political system, but it did not materialize because of endless party rivalry and a guerrilla war in Cuba in favor of the island's independence. Troops were sent from Madrid to quell the uprising, and the government had to abandon two commitments—the ending of conscription and food taxes—that had given the Revolution popular backing. The Cortes (parliament) replaced Isabella with Amadeo I, the son of King Victor Emmanuel of Italy, who reigned for less than three years (1870–1873). Prim was assassinated on the very day Amadeo entered Madrid. The king abdicated after failing to form a stable government, and the Cortes declared a republic.

Why was the First Spanish Republic (1873–1874) short lived?

Spain's First Republic was born on February 11, 1873, at a time of mounting political instability and social unrest. The country was sinking into chaos: the third Carlist war raged mainly in the north of Spain, Barcelona pushed for autonomy, anarchists whipped up violence in the south, and convents and priests were attacked in anticlerical violence. Idle or underused church land had been expropriated during the first Carlist war in an unsuccessful bid to encourage production by small landowners, and the 1869 Constitution had admitted religious freedom, although Catholicism remained the official state religion. The church also had political representation through a number of seats in the senate and much latitude with regard to religious orders (the number of monks in Spain rose from about 1,500 to more than 22,000 in 1910).

The Republic was initially a federation of 17 areas. It later fragmented even further as a result of Cantonalism, or extreme localism. By the summer of 1873 several cities, including Valencia, Malaga, and Granada, had declared their independence from Madrid. The English writer Richard Ford had noted in his *Handbook for Travellers in Spain*, first published in 1845, that Spain was a "bundle of local units tied together by a rope of sand." Ford said Spain was the country of the *patria chica*. *Patria* (country) is first and foremost a place of origin and *chica* means little and hence something to be protected. A Spaniard's first loyalty is often to the village, town, or city where he was born, a tangible place, and not to his country: these feelings are expressed in the tens of thousands of annual fiestas that take place in villages.

In just 11 months Spain had four presidents, until General Manuel Pavía rebelled in Madrid and established a unified republic led by Francisco Serrano. This republic was, in turn, ended almost a year later by another coup d'état under General Arsenio Martínez-Campos at Sagunto. The army had ended the Bourbon monarchy in Spain seven years earlier, when Isabella was knocked off the throne, and it now restored it with Alfonso XII (1874–1885). The army had decided that it was its duty to "save" the country from chaos; the next time this argument was invoked was in 1936, when General Franco's uprising plunged the country into a three-year civil war.

What was the "Disaster" of 1898?

The restored Bourbon monarchy, aided by the constitution of 1876 and universal male suffrage, brought a period of relative stability of alternating governments formed by the Liberal and Conservative parties. The political system, however, did not fit the socioeconomic reality of a predominantly rural and illiterate country. The alternation in power between narrow political elites was called the *turno pacífico* and was based on corrupt electoral practices. Elections were generally rigged by local *caciques* (powerful figures in rural areas). Nevertheless, the country advanced until the Spanish-American War in 1898, which resulted in the loss of the colonies of Cuba, Puerto Rico, and the Philippines, the remnants of the formerly vast empire.

American public opinion grew angrier at Spanish mistreatment of rebels fighting against the colonial rule and pushed President William McKinley into war with Spain. The humiliating Spanish defeat, still known today as *El Desastre* (the Disaster), caused a profound psychological shock at home and triggered a period of introspection during the reign of Alfonso XIII (1886–1931), examining the reasons for the country's backwardness. The military officer corps blamed the civilian government for its defeat and began to view the political class as an internal threat.

The self-image of Spain as a great power was shattered: while the American colonies had been lost in a civil war between metropolitan and colonial Spaniards, Cuba was snatched by a foreign power and at a time when imperial powers like Britain were furthering their interests and new ones such as Germany and Italy were emerging. The loss of Cuba, the jewel in what was left of the imperial crown, was a particularly severe blow for Catalonia, more than half of whose exports (cotton garments, shoes, leather goods) were sold to the island. By 1900, they had ceased to exist. The defeat also left the bloated army, a caste that was idle and without a mission, turning inward and looking for a new role.

The leading lights of the loose but influential intellectual and political movement known as the "generation of '98" included Joaquín Costa, the educationist Francisco Giner de los Ríos, the poet Antonio Machado and the novelist Pío Baroja. Costa was the leading figure of a movement known as *regeneracionismo* (regenerationism); he called for an "iron surgeon" (a strongman) to sort out Spain's problems. Giner de los Ríos promoted a version of the Protestant ethic of self-improvement and tolerance. He and others founded in 1876 the Institución Libre de Enseñanza (Free Institute of Education). This was initially a kind of university independent of the church and of the government, but it did not give degrees. It later turned into a network of primary and secondary schools of considerable influence among the liberal elite. This was followed by the creation of the Residencia de Estudiantes (Student Residence) in 1910 that also played a major role in intellectual life for the next 25 years. At one point, the poet Federico García Lorca, the painter Salvador Dali, and the filmmaker Luis Buñuel were all at the Residencia. Santiago Ramón y Cajal, the Nobel laureate for medicine in 1906, fostered scientific and intellectual development through the Junta para la Ampliación de Estudios e Investigaciones Científicas (the Council for the Extension of Studies and Scientific Research), which enabled bright Spaniards to carry on studying abroad.

The liberal philosopher José Ortega y Gasset wrote in 1910, "Spain is the problem, Europe is the solution." He was referring to a constant of Spanish history—the inability to be in step with liberal democratic Europe. It was a visionary statement that became the constant mantra of successive generations of liberal Spaniards seeking to modernize the country right up to 1986, when Spain joined the European Union.

Why did Alfonso XIII go into exile in 1931?

The period between 1898 and 1931, when the Second Republic was established, saw attempts at "reform from above" by the politicians of the Restoration (the period that began after the ending of the First Republic in 1874 and the restoration of the Bourbon monarchy) and rising "revolution from below." Alfonso XIII, who assumed control of the state in 1902 when he was 16, was perfectly aware of his responsibility, stating, "On me depends whether Spain is to remain a Bourbon monarchy or become a Republic."

The politicians from the Conservative, Liberal, and Republican parties hoped social and political reforms would stem the growing discontent. But there was no common ground and little agreement within the parties themselves, as they were wrought by factionalism. There were more than ten governments between 1898 and 1923. The badge of identity of the right, which wanted to turn back the clock, was defense of the privileges of the church, increasingly under attack for its wealth and social and educational influence, while the nonviolent left, among other things, saw a modern educational system as the key to a modern society. The clerical right wanted obligatory religious instruction in state secondary schools and full freedom from state control in their own schools. Liberals sought respect for liberty of conscience and state control over private-sector secondary education.

The country became bogged down in an unpopular military conflict in the Spanish protectorate of Morocco as the army sought to regain the prestige it had lost in the 1898 Spanish-American War and expand its influence in North Africa, while keeping the coastline opposite Spain out of French hands. The calling up of reserve troops in 1909 sparked what became known as the *Semana Trágica* (Tragic Week) in Barcelona and other Catalan cities, during which workers confronted the army. More than 100 people were killed in the clashes. Anarchists set fire to convents and churches.

A year later anarchists established the Confederación Nacional de Trabajo (National Confederation of Labor, CNT) in the Catalan capital of Barcelona and they joined the Unión General de Trabajadores (General Union of Workers, UGT), the more moderate trade union of the Socialists founded in 1888, in pressing for better working and living conditions. The two unions quickly became rivals, however. They drew support from discontented workers who had moved from the countryside, where food was often scarce, to cities in search of work. At least half of the workforce was employed in the agriculture sector. It is estimated that between 1900 and 1913, 1.5 million

Spaniards moved to cities such as Barcelona, Bilbao, and Madrid or emigrated, particularly from the poorest regions, such as Andalusia and Galicia. Land in the former was mainly made up of huge estates run by a few wealthy families and in the latter consisted of tiny plots.

The 1914–1918 World War, during which Spain was neutral, closed off the escape valve of emigration, producing more migration to cities and swelling their populations. The war was good for industrialists and ship owners as exports boomed, but the benefits did not trickle down to the impoverished masses. Political violence, inspired by the 1917 Russian Revolution, gripped some cities, particularly Barcelona, where there was open warfare between the CNT and the right-wing Free Syndicates, who were backed by employers and were part of the Catholic labor movement. Elements of the army were also unhappy; in 1917 a labor union of some officers, known as the *juntas de defensa*, demanded better pay and promotion by seniority and not by their record of fighting in Morocco. In 1921, the Spanish army suffered another "disaster" at the battle of Anual in the Rif region, when Berber tribesmen killed some 8,000 soldiers, most of them conscripts. Spanish aircraft dropped mustard gas in the Rif war. Parliament demanded an investigation into the responsibility of Alfonso XIII, who had directed the campaign from Madrid, and of the notoriously corrupt armed forces.

General Miguel Primo de Rivera, an aristocrat, seized power in 1923, just before the results of the investigation were due to be presented to parliament. This ended almost 50 years without military intervention and the corrupt *turno* system of alternating governments. Alfonso acted outside of the constitution and named Primo de Rivera head of the Directorio Militar (Military Directory), thereby implicitly supporting the coup d'état. This alienated the king from all the politicians in parliament, particularly the Socialists, as well as intellectuals. The authoritarian Primo de Rivera, seen as the "iron surgeon" called for by Joaquín Costa, announced his aim was to "open a brief parenthesis in the constitutional life of Spain and re-establish it as soon as the country offers us men uncontaminated with the vices of political organization." The parenthesis lasted seven years.

Alfonso took a backseat, while Primo de Rivera launched a plan of industrialization and public works, which considerably improved the roads, created reservoirs, and extended the electric power system. He also set up the semi-state Banco Exterior to finance foreign trade, nationalized the telephone company owned by the US ITT, and established the Campsa oil monopoly and the network of state-owned hotels, often in restored castles and palaces, known as *paradores*. These hotels are still very popular today. The economic boom petered out toward the end of the 1920s, the peseta plunged against foreign currencies, inflation was high, and a poor harvest aggravated the lack of sufficient food supply.

The increasingly unpopular Primo de Rivera also fell afoul of the artillery officer class over the issue of promotions. Alfonso, portrayed in a clandestine pamphlet as a "dancing partner" of Primo de Rivera, sought an opportunity to disassociate the monarchy from what in effect was a personal dictatorship and make amends for having supported it. When Primo de Rivera canvassed the army in 1930 to gauge his support and found that he had lost it, the king did not hesitate in accepting his resignation.

General Berenguer, a known enemy of Primo de Rivera and identified with the conservative status quo, became prime minister with the mission of returning Spain to constitutional government after calling general elections. Berenguer ruled by decree and censorship for a year, delaying the elections, which were never held. Alfonso became more and more unpopular in almost every quarter. A revolt led by army officers in Jaca, following an alliance of anti-Alfonso forces established by the Pact of San Sebastian, failed to rally support, and the rebels were captured and executed.

Municipal elections were held on April 12, 1931, as the first step back to constitutional normality. A majority of provincial capitals (46 out of 50) voted for republican parties, though the majority of councilors in Spain were monarchists, thereby winning support from smaller towns. The country was split, at least electorally, between a countryside that mainly voted monarchist and large towns in favor of a republic. Two days later the king declared that the elections "have shown me that I no longer enjoy the love of my people." The king had particularly lost the support of the army and the Civil Guard. He boarded a ship for France and left Spain. Thus ended the Bourbon dynasty after 231 years. It did not return until 1975, when Alfonso XIII's grandson, Juan Carlos, succeeded General Franco as head of state.

What were the causes of the 1936–1939 Civil War?

The Second Republic, born in the depths of the world slump, sounded the death knell for the corrupt system of alternating governments based on rigged elections and a limited electorate. It ushered in mass politics in a country whose rate of illiteracy and level of economic development was similar to that of England in the 1830s and France in the 1860s. Spain's first taste of genuine parliamentary democracy came 150 years after the US Constitution and a century after the Reform Act in Britain. Over the next five years, the supporters of six opposing forces competed for power: liberal democracy, authoritarian conservatism, fascism, regional nationalism, socialism, and communism, which at the time of the outbreak of the Civil War was weak.

Elections in June 1931 gave a large majority in the parliament to supporters of the Republic, who immediately began to redistribute power by reforming land ownership, the education system, church-state relations, and the army. Among the first measures were an autonomy statute for Catalonia, approved in a referendum, and a raft of labor legislation concerning sickness benefits, the eight-hour day, minimum wages, and a mechanism for settling labor disputes. After centuries of neglect, an ambitious program for the construction of schools and the training of teachers was also instituted. In December 1931 a new constitution, modeled on other "progressive" ones, including the Mexican constitution of 1917 and the Weimar constitution of 1919, introduced female suffrage, civil marriage, and divorce, and established free, obligatory, and secular education. Articles 24 and 26 inflamed the upholders of the *ancien régime*, as they separated church and state, prohibited the religious orders from teaching, and removed the crucifix from state schools, alienating the social classes whose children had traditionally attended them. The church had thousands of religious communities, with more than 100,000 priests, monks, and nuns. The Jesuit order was banned in 1932.

The philosopher José Ortega y Gasset said these clauses were "exploding cartridges" capable of shattering the Republic's stability. Some churches and convents were burned. For the anticlerical left, the church and big landowners were the enemies of social and economic modernization and democracy and had to be tamed. (The answer in a catechism of the time to the question "what kind of sin is committed by one who votes for a liberal candidate?" was "generally a mortal one.") In Andalusia, 1 percent of owners controlled more than 40 percent of the land, much of which was idle. A kind of feudalism lasted longer in Spain than in any other Western European country. Luis Buñuel's 1933 surreal documentary film *Las Hurdes: Tierra Sin Pan* (Las Hurdes: Land without Bread) graphically depicts rural poverty in northern Extremadura.

The Republic was divided from the outset. Conservative republicans wanted a modern capitalist state, while anarchists were bent on destroying it. The aggressive measures against the church (even the ringing of church bells was restricted in some areas) led to the resignation in October 1931 of Niceto Alcalá Zamora, the provisional president, and Miguel Maura, the interior minister. There were divisions in the left and even within the Socialist Party over strategy. The right had more interests in common; persecution of the church became a rallying point for opposition to the Republic.

After the abortive coup d'état in August 1932 of General José Sanjurjo, known as the Lion of the Rif because of the reputation for bravery he had gained in the wars in Morocco, the right sought to regain power by working within the system. José María Gil Robles, a Catholic lawyer, established the Confederación Española de Derechas Autónomas (CEDA; Spanish Confederation of Autonomous Right-Wing Groups), a broad right-wing confessional alliance that aimed to win power through the ballot box and reverse the reforms through "a true and deep revolution with the cross in hand." (By then an authoritarian regime in Austria had been established.) Gil Robles's followers hailed him as *Jefe* (leader) and displayed portraits of him 10 meters high. Businessmen and landowners took their capital out of the country, severely weakening the peseta against foreign currencies. Discontent gathered pace in urban and rural areas, leading to clashes between protesting workers and Republican security forces, most notably at Casas Viejas in Andalusia. About 25 people died.

The supporters of the Republic did not overcome their differences by the time of the November 1933 elections, which extended the franchise to more than six million women, and unlike the right the left-wing parties did not campaign on a joint ticket. They paid a heavy price: the nine right-wing parties won 242 seats (115 of them CEDA's), giving them an absolute majority, the eight parties of the left obtained 100 (58 of them Socialist), and the center won 131. The Communists, who were to play a dominant role during the Civil War, had just one seat, while José Antonio Primo de Rivera, the founder of the fascist Falange that year and the son of the general who was prime minister between 1923 and 1930, entered parliament under the CEDA's ticket.

The CEDA initially backed the minority government of the Radical Republicans and in October 1934 entered the government, triggering a revolt in Asturias led by militant miners.

The army brutally suppressed the revolt. The failure of the uprising in Asturias, the suspension of land reform and of the Catalan statute, and other measures that turned back the clock radicalized the left, particularly the Socialists. The country was very polarized: anticlericals opposed the church, while the unions opposed the landed classes and the republicans vied against the monarchists.

Having learned the bitter lesson of disunity in the 1933 election, the Socialist and Communist parties, the Republican Union, and other supporters of the Republic, including two Catalan parties, formed a Popular Front for the February 1936 election. Francisco Largo Caballero, the Socialist leader, declared that if the right won again "we must of necessity move to civil war" while Gil Robles's electoral propaganda was equally extremist in announcing, "For God and Country: to conquer or die." The political center was weak.

The Popular Front won 278 seats in parliament (99 of them Socialist), the National Front 137 (88 of them CEDA), and centrist parties 56. The tally of votes, however, was very close (4.6 million and 4.5 million, respectively). The left's strongholds were cities, industrial areas, and the south of the country, where rural unemployment among landless peasants was very high, while the right controlled central Spain. The CEDA's strategy of using the system as a Trojan horse to overthrow it had not worked. It became discredited among the most reactionary forces and outflanked by two more extreme parties, the National Block of the monarchist José Calvo Sotelo and the Falange. The military coup option gained strength; generals began to plot.

The Popular Front government of Manuel Azaña granted an amnesty for political prisoners, restored Catalan autonomy, and moved generals suspected of plotting against the Republic, such as Franco, to remote posts (in his case the Canary Islands). Street violence in Madrid spiraled out of control. On July 13, after a Falangist killed a Republican guard the day before, Calvo Sotelo was arrested at home, and his body was found at the gates of a Madrid cemetery in a revenge killing.

It was the final straw in what the philosopher Julián Marías termed a "collective madness" resulting from "the social fabric being torn apart by a relentless pull from both political extremes."⁴ Several military garrisons, beginning with Melilla, the Spanish enclave on the North African coast, rose on July 17 and 18, sparking a protracted civil war that pitted centrists against regionalists, religious believers against secularizers, cosmopolitan urbanites against rural traditionalists, and involved different classes and political ideologies. An estimated 14,000 officers supported the uprising and 8,500 remained loyal to the Republic. One of the first leading Republican figures to be killed was the universally known poet Federico García Lorca, who was arrested in Granada by henchmen loyal to Franco and executed by the side of a lonely country road. The search for his grave after the end of the Franco dictatorship became something of a crusade among the left.

Who was General Francisco Franco?

General Franco, who staged the coup d'état against the Republic in 1936 and triggered the three-year Civil War, was Spain's dictator until he died in 1975. The son of a naval postmaster, he was born six years before the "Disaster" of 1898 in El Ferrol, Galicia, an area that sharply felt the loss of the remnants of the empire (Cuba, the Philippines, and Puerto Rico), as it was the port city of some of the ships sunk in the Spanish-American War. Frustrated in his ambition to join the navy, when he was 15 Franco entered the infantry academy at Toledo, an institution that was deeply influenced by the loss of the last colonies and which blamed the political class for Spain's decline. In 1917, he led a unit that helped put down a strike in Oviedo, Asturias. He then spent ten years in Spanish North Africa fighting a colonial war, where he gained a reputation for leadership, discipline, bravery, and ruthlessness. He rose quickly through the ranks and by the time he was 33 was the youngest general in Europe since Napoleon.

His time in Africa formed his mind-set; "without Africa I cannot explain myself to myself or to my comrades in arms." In 1927, he became head of Spain's main military academy at Zaragoza, which he turned into a hotbed of the ultranationalist and reactionary right. When workers in Asturias rose against the entry of the right-wing CEDA into the Republican government in October 1934, Franco sent troops from the Foreign Legion and Moroccan mercenaries to the region and commanded them from the ministry of war in Madrid. The rebellion was crushed at the cost of 1,500 dead, 3,000 wounded, and 25,000 arrested. He called in these forces, as he had commanded and trusted them, unlike mainland soldiers, in Africa. Visiting Oviedo, the capital of Asturias, after his victory, he described the uprising as a "frontier war, and at the frontiers are socialism and communism, which are attacking civilization in order to replace it by barbarism." He saw himself as destined to "save Spain" in the line of national heroes such as El Cid. Supporters of the Republic and their ideas were alien to the "true" Spain, and he equated them with the Berbers in North Africa, as both in his eyes were rebels.

Franco was not particularly religious as a young man but became so after he married Carmen Polo, a minor aristocrat. When he was installed in the Pardo Palace near Madrid after his Civil War victory, he kept beside his bed the mummified arm of St. Teresa of Avila. According to traditional Catholic mythology, St. Teresa's body was incorrupt. In September 1936, less than two months after the military coup, the junta of generals proclaimed Franco head of government, and he gave himself the title head of state. He was also generalissimo of the armed forces (Joseph Stalin had the same title) and head of the Movimiento Nacional (National Movement), the only legal political organization. Shortly after his victory, Franco proclaimed that he had "liquidated the nineteenth century, which should never have existed," as the liberalism attempted was "the negation of the Spanish spirit." He claimed his victory had been ordained by God and by history. According to the inscription on coinage during his regime, he was "Caudillo of Spain by the Grace of God."

What were the ideological dimensions of the Civil War?

The Spanish Civil War is seen as a prelude to the ideological battles of the Second World War between fascism, communism, and democracy, which was sparked by Germany's invasion of Poland seven months after General Franco's victory in April 1939, although the Civil War involved many issues that were specific to Spain, such as religious cleavage and regional nationalism. For the first time since the Napoleonic invasion of Spain (1808–1814), Spain was caught up in a broader struggle that transcended its borders. The Nationalist rebels fought for a restoration of the traditional order, most notably the position of the Catholic Church, while supporters of the Republic were divided as the war progressed between defending liberal democracy and communist revolution. The fact that Hitler's Nazi Germany and Mussolini's fascist Italy supported Franco and Stalin's Communist Soviet Union backed the Republic accentuated the ideological dimension.

The church blessed Franco's cause, calling it a crusade. Enrique Plá y Deniel, the Bishop of Salamanca, the capital at the time of the Nationalist-held territory, issued a pastoral letter in September 1936 in which he said the conflict was part of a global struggle. "On the soil of Spain a bloody conflict is being waged between two conceptions of life, two forces preparing for universal conflict in every country...Communists and Anarchists are sons of Cain, fratricides, assassins of those who cultivate virtue." The church reduced the very complex circumstances to a black-and-white struggle between good and evil.

What role did foreign intervention play in the Civil War?

The Civil War was internationalized right from the start. Fascist Italy and Nazi Germany supplied transport planes that enabled General Franco's troops, the best equipped, to cross from Morocco to mainland Spain at the start of the war. Italy provided 70,000 troops and Germany sent 5,000 advisors and the Condor Legion of around 100 aircraft and pilots. The Civil War gave Hitler, in particular, an opportunity to try out new weapons and techniques. On April 26, 1937, during market day, 60 German and Italian aircraft dropped blast and incendiary bombs (designed to burn at 2,500°C) on the town of Guernica, the ancient center of Basque rights and liberties, in one of the first aerial bombardments of a defenseless civilian population in Europe. Several hundred people were killed.

The Soviet Union, in particular, and Mexico, to a lesser extent, came to the rescue of the Republic. Moscow sent 2,000 advisors and held considerable sway over the government as the war progressed. The Republic paid for Soviet support by shipping 500 tons of gold from the vaults of the Bank of Spain (the central bank) to the Soviet Union. The democracies of the United States, Britain, and France adopted a policy of nonintervention, which meant Spain could not buy arms from these governments. The Socialist government of France was initially in favor of supporting its brethren in Spain, but could not do so without the acquiescence of Britain, which was still seeking to appease Hitler.

The Republic, to a much greater extent than Franco's side, also attracted 60,000 volunteer fighters from abroad who enlisted in the International Brigades. Women volunteers worked as nurses. Many of the foreigners who defended the Republic were exiles from authoritarian European countries who saw an opportunity to fight for causes lost in their own country. About one-quarter of the *brigadistas* were Jewish. The war also attracted European and American left-wing intellectuals. The British Socialist writer George Orwell fought with the anti-Stalinist Partido Obrero de Unificación Marxista (United Marxist Workers' Party, POUM). Pro-Stalin communists labeled the POUM "Trotskyist" and claimed it had been infiltrated by Fascist agents provocateurs and was part of Franco's "fifth column." (Leon Trotsky was assassinated in Mexico in 1940 on Stalin's orders.) The British poet W. H. Auden (1907–1973) broadcast Republican propaganda in Spain for several weeks and gave all the royalties from the sale of his politically engaged poem "Spain" (1937) to Medical Aid for Spain.[5] Among the foreign correspondents covering the war was Ernest Hemingway. Orwell's formative experiences in Spain, recounted in *Homage to Catalonia*, shaped his political outlook and made him a vociferous opponent of all totalitarian systems. They also played a part in the inspiration behind his masterpieces, *Animal Farm* (published in 1945) and *Nineteen Eighty-Four* (1949). Orwell escaped Spain when he and his wife came under threat from Spanish Communists and agents of the Communist International (Comintern). The POUM leader, Andreu Nin, a former secretary of Trotsky, was less lucky: he was arrested, tortured, and murdered.

Why did the Republicans lose the Civil War?

The rebels against the democratically elected Republic had might on their side, particularly superior airpower, thanks to the support of Hitler's Germany and Mussolini's Italy. Not only did General Franco's armed forces have better weapons and greater experience of battles, gained in North Africa, they were also better disciplined and under a single military and political command, unlike the forces of the Republic. Franco's army also managed its conscripts (1.2 million) better than the Republican Popular Army (1.7 million). Nationalist soldiers fought under better material conditions and suffered fewer shortages in the front line.

Effective administration on the Republican side was hampered by the deep rift at the government level between the Socialists and Communists, while on the ground factionalism among the left produced a kind of civil war within a civil war. For example, factions fought each other in the streets of Barcelona in May 1937 after the Communist Party and its Catalan branch tried to take over an anarchist-controlled telephone exchange.

Liberal Republicans were alienated by the anticlerical violence perpetrated by anarchists and other groups apparently beyond the government's control: 13 bishops and 6,832 priests, nuns, monks, and other religious personnel were killed compared to around 900 clerics during the French Revolution. Historians have called this the largest clerical bloodletting in the history of the Christian Church. In some towns, almost the entire clergy was eliminated. (Among the Republican supporters, a disproportionate number of teachers were murdered.) Around 1,000 Spanish "martyrs" were later beatified or canonized by John Paul II (1978–2005) and Benedict XVI (2005–2013).

As the war dragged on, the Republicans faced a growing shortage of troops and frenetically resorted to increasingly unpopular conscription. Seventeen-year-olds called up in the last months of the war in 1939 were known collectively as the Quinta del Biberón, or the "Feeding-bottle reserve class." Food was also scarce in the Republican-held areas, sapping morale, as the grain-producing territories in central Spain were under Franco's control and his blockade of the Mediterranean coast prevented imports from getting through.

2

THE FRANCO REGIME, 1939–1975

What kind of dictatorship did General Franco establish after winning the 1936–1939 Civil War?

On top of the more than 200,000 who died at the battle fronts between 1936 and 1939, at least 150,000 people were murdered extrajudicially or executed after flimsy legal process in the Nationalist-held areas and 50,000 were killed in the Republican territories, out of a population of 24 million.[1] More than 250,000 Spaniards went into permanent exile, including much of Spain's professional and intellectual classes, depriving the country of some of its best brains, and 33,000 children were shipped by their Republican parents during the Civil War to the Soviet Union, Mexico, Britain, and other countries. Far from seeking reconciliation, Franco carried on the repression in order to purify the country of those deemed to be its enemies. He created a victory culture, which divided Spain into winners and losers throughout the dictatorship. The regime was based on adherents to it being favored over non-adherents. Participation in it was reserved for the first group. The date of the uprising that sparked the Civil War (July 18) and that of Franco's victory (April 1) were turned into official commemorations and national holidays. An extra week's wages was given in July in the public and private sectors, known as the *paga del 18 de Julio* (the July 18 payment).

The Law of Political Responsibilities, promulgated in February 1939, two months before the war ended and retroactive to October 1, 1934, the date of the revolt of Asturian miners, together with the Law for the Repression of Freemasonry and Communism of March 1940, enabled the regime to imprison or execute people who, "blinded by an incomprehensible sectarianism, commit actions or omissions that might prejudice this Movement of Redemption of the Fatherland." The Bellón Commission, named after Ildefonso Bellón, the president of the Nationalist Supreme Court, had concluded in February 1939 that the military uprising of July 1936 "cannot in any sense be defined as a rebellion," as the Republican government was "fundamentally and strictly illegitimate." It even claimed that King Alfonso XIII was "overthrown" after monarchists had won the 1931 municipal elections. According to this inverse justice, defense of the Republic in any form constituted rebellion. At least 20,000 people were executed during the first half of the 1940s, mostly after military trials, more than the number of political enemies killed during and after the liberation of France and Italy at the end of World War II (fascists, collaborators, etc.). By November 1940, more than 280,000 people were in prison and entire professions were cleansed: an estimated 60,000 schoolteachers, suspected of Republican sympathies, had to prove their loyalty to the regime in order to be able to teach. In 1940 the regime's Information and Investigation Service gathered information on the political background of more than 2.9 million people out of a population of 25.8 million. The first years of the regime were so brutal that Dionisio Ridruejo, the director of Franco's propaganda machine and later a left-of-center opponent of the regime, said of this period: "Morally, the conquered became the victors."

The poet Antonio Machado (1875–1939), who died in exile in France five weeks before the war ended, published this prophetic lullaby for newborns almost 20 years before the conflict:

> Little Spanish child, may God protect you.
> One of the two Spains is sure to try to still your heart.

Other well-known figures who died in exile included the journalist Manuel Chaves Nogales in London in 1944, the composer Manuel de Falla in Argentina in 1946, the writer Arturo Barea, author of the trilogy *The Forging of a Rebel*, in England in 1957, the poet and Nobel laureate Juan Ramón Jiménez in Puerto Rico in 1958, and the film director Luis Buñuel, whose *Le charme discret de la bourgeoisie* (The Discreet Charm of the Bourgeoisie) won an Oscar (in 1973), in Mexico in 1983.

Several thousand Republican and common prisoners were put to work between 1940 and 1959 building the Valley of the Fallen monument in the Guadarrama Mountains near Madrid. Thousands of people killed in the Civil War were buried there. The monument includes a basilica tunneled into the mountain and crowned by a 150-meter-high cross. It was inaugurated by Franco, who asked rhetorically, "What are the enemies of Spain?" He answered, "The enemies of Spain are seven: liberalism, democracy, Judaism, the Masons, capitalism, Marxism, and separatism." On one side of the altar is the tomb of José Antonio Primo de Rivera, the founder of the fascist Falange, executed on November 20, 1936, by Republicans. Franco died in 1975 on the same day as Primo de Rivera, giving the date an almost mystical significance for his supporters, and was buried opposite him on the other side of the altar. He is the only person in the basilica who died a natural death. The use of political prisoners for forced labor continued until 1970.

Francoist monuments were also erected in many towns. Those who died fighting on his side, "for God and Spain," were remembered with church plaques bearing their names and the Catholic monarchs' crest of the yoke and arrows, the symbol adopted by the Falange and representing Spanish unity. Republicans were buried in common graves, which did not begin to be publicly unearthed until well after the end of the dictatorship. Streets were renamed after Civil War generals; the most prominent ones often bore the name of Primo de Rivera. The totemic date of July 18—the date of Franco's uprising—was commemorated every year and there was a parade every April 1 to celebrate the victory. The autonomy enjoyed by Catalonia (as of 1932) and the Basque Country (as of July 1936) came to an end. The speaking of the regional languages was outlawed, as were innocuous activities such as regional dance and music. While living in Barcelona during the 1950s as a young research student, Sir John Elliott, the distinguished British historian, made the mistake of asking a traffic policeman for directions in Catalan instead of Castilian. His response was *Hable la lengua del imperio* ("Speak the language of the empire"). Spaniards could not even ask for an *ensaladilla rusa* (potato salad), as it referenced Russia, which supported the Republic during the Civil War. The name of the dish was officially changed to *ensaladilla imperial*.

The freedoms enjoyed by women during the Second Republic (1931–1939), including divorce and the right to vote, were also reversed. The regime declared civil marriages that had taken place during the Second Republic void, thereby making thousands of children retrospectively illegitimate. The law discriminated strongly against married women. Article 57 of the penal code (repealed in 1975) stated that "The husband must protect his wife and she must obey her husband." Without her husband's approval, a wife was prohibited from almost all economic activities, including employment, ownership of property, or even travel away from home. The law also provided for less stringent definitions of such crimes as adultery and desertion for husbands than it did for wives. Single women were not allowed to leave their home without their parents' consent before the age of 25.

What was the Franco regime's role in the Second World War, and what happened to it after the defeat of Nazism?

The Second World War began six months after Franco's Civil War victory in April 1939. The dictator took the side of the Axis powers, with whom he identified ideologically although Spain was officially neutral. Hitler met Franco at Hendaye in October 1940 to try to persuade him to directly enter the war or allow the Third Reich free passage through Spain. Hitler wanted to seize the strategically important British territory of Gibraltar, which is located at the southern tip of the peninsula with a commanding position at the western gateway to the Mediterranean. After the meeting Hitler told Mussolini in a letter that he would "prefer to have three or four teeth pulled than meet Franco again." Franco wanted too much, including Gibraltar and a large part of the French colonial empire in Africa, and had little to give in exchange, at least militarily. Had Hitler controlled the Mediterranean, this would have changed the course of the Second World War.

The regime's main contribution to Hitler's war effort was to send the División Azul (Blue Division, named after the blue shirts of the Falange) of 18,000 volunteers to fight on the Eastern Front in 1941. This expedition also allowed Franco to rid himself of young radical elements in the Falange. The regime also exported wolfram, a key element for the manufacturing of armaments, and other minerals to Germany and allowed U-boats to enter Spanish ports. The Bank of Spain, the country's central bank, received Nazi gold, some of it looted from Holocaust victims. As in the Civil War, Spaniards found themselves on opposite sides in the Second World War. Some of the troops fighting with the Soviet forces against the Nazis were exiled Spaniards who had remained in the Soviet Union after the Civil War ended. Close to 300 of these exiles, some of whom were shipped to the Soviet Union as children during the Civil War, were imprisoned in gulags between 1939 and 1956 for various "crimes." These included trying to leave the

Soviet Union for Spain or another country, often in order to be reunited with their families, or for being regarded as dissidents.[2] The Communist authorities rarely allowed them to leave. The Spanish Communist Party leadership in Moscow was complicit in this repression. In essence, these people were regarded as "traitors" to the Communist paradise.

Other Republican supporters who had fled across the border into France fought in the Resistance against the German occupation forces. Lluis Companys, the president of the Generalitat, the Catalan government, was captured by the Gestapo in France and returned to Spain, where he was executed in 1940. Francisco Largo Caballero, the Socialist president of the Republic in 1936, spent four years in the Sachsenhausen concentration camp near Berlin. Around 10,000 Spaniards died in Nazi concentration camps, half of them in Mauthausen. One of the prisoners in this camp was the Catalan Francesc Boix, who worked in the SS photographic service and hid around 2,000 photos. He testified as a key witness in the 1945–1946 Nuremberg trials. Several hundred Spaniards fought with the French 2nd Armored Division commanded by General Philippe Leclerc, which liberated Paris in August 1944. The German governor of Paris surrendered to a Spanish soldier before he signed the capitulation of his forces.

The victory of the Allies left Franco's regime a pariah. In March 1946, the United States, Britain, and France declared that Spain could not look forward to "full and cordial association" with them as long as Franco remained in power. The ostracism was designed to bring about "a peaceful withdrawal of Franco, the abolition of the Falange, and the establishment of an interim or caretaker government under which the Spanish people may have an opportunity freely to determine the type of government they wish to have." Franco did not budge and held a referendum in July 1947 on the law of succession, which declared Spain a "traditional, Catholic, social and representative monarchy," with Franco as king in all but name and with the right to appoint his successor. A year later Spain was excluded from the Marshall Plan, the US aid program that helped to rebuild 16 non-communist economies in postwar Europe. This rejection was amusingly satirized in Luis García Berlanga's famous 1953 film *Bienvenido Mr. Marshall* (Welcome Mr. Marshall), whose subtleties escaped Franco's censors. One of the scenes shows a large American car speeding through a village and passing crowds, leaving nothing in its trail but dust and dashed hopes. It was not made clear whether Mr. Marshall was in the car.

How was the regime organized politically?

The only legal political organization was the Movimiento Nacional (National Movement), which grew out of the Falange Española Tradicionalista y de las Juntas de Ofensiva Nacional Sindicalista (the Spanish Traditional Phalanx and of the Assemblies of the National Syndicalist Offensive), an amalgamation in 1937 of the political forces that supported the military uprising. The Falange did not win a single seat in the February 1936 general election, the last one before the Civil War. Franco, however, chose it as the vehicle for the regime's ideology and the source of its politicians. Its founder, José Antonio Primo de Rivera, whom Franco always saw as a rival, was executed in 1936 after the Civil War began and became a martyr-hero. Like Franco, the Falange blamed the liberalism of the 19th century for Spain's decline and regarded political parties as alien to the true Spain. "A century and a half of parliamentary democracy," Franco said, "accompanied by the loss of immense territory, three civil wars, and the imminent danger of national disintegration, add up to a disastrous balance sheet, sufficient to discredit parliamentary systems in the eyes of the Spanish people."

The Francoist state was based on "organic democracy" (a parliamentary democracy was "inorganic"), in which people were represented not by political parties, which, in the regime's words, "sacrifice the interests of the nation to those of the party," but by "natural" institutions, such as municipalities, the family, and "vertical" trade unions (known as *sindicatos*). Although the state initially proclaimed itself "a totalitarian instrument in the service of the national integrity," it came to be more authoritarian than totalitarian after 1957, according to the US-based Spanish sociologist Juan Linz, who elaborated the concept of the authoritarian regime precisely in order to define the Franco dictatorship. Within the regime, which also embraced Bourbon and Carlist monarchists who accepted the legitimacy of Franco's rule, there was what Linz called "limited pluralism" among the various political "families." The dictatorship was more one of an authoritarian regime run by a military man than a military dictatorship in the full sense of the word. Franco regarded himself as being responsible only to "God and History." The regime was a far cry from the totalitarian regimes of Nazi Germany and the Communist Soviet Union, although, like them, it could be merciless against anyone who opposed it.

Workers and employers formed trade unions, founded in 1940 on the pattern of Mussolini's corporations. Each one was made up of everyone in a given branch of production. They were aimed at solving the problem of class conflict; separate organizations, as in a parliamentary democracy, were not needed in the eyes of the state because everyone was working for the best interests of the nation.

The Falange organized women through its Sección Femenina (Women's Section), established by Pilar, the sister of Primo de Rivera. All single women between the ages of 18 and 35 had to complete six months' social service, where they were told to aspire to marriage and motherhood and expect little else. In the final years of the dictatorship, when social and political unrest intensified, political associations were authorized. The only groups to take advantage of this were those loyal to the regime.

Political control was also exercised through the press, which was a "fourth estate," ranking in importance after the National Movement, the state-run trade unions, and the political police (the Brigada Politico-Social). Like these institutions, the role of the Spanish media emerged out of the Civil War and was designed to keep the flag of Franco's "crusade" flying and serve the regime, particularly the state-run television and radio. One of the stipulations of the Federation of Press Associations under Franco ran: "As Spaniards brought up in the Catholic faith and as defenders of the glorious National Movement, our duty is to serve with zeal these religious and political truths...." The Movement built up a network of 38 newspapers and 40 radio stations. The newspapers had far more influence than that indicated by their total circulation (around 450,000), particularly in rural areas (in 11 provinces the only newspaper available belonged to the Movement). The official press also included the newspaper *Pueblo*, the organ of the state-run trade unions, and the far-right *El Alcazar*, named after the fortress in Toledo (today an army museum) where Nationalist forces were besieged by Republican forces at the start of the Civil War and famously held out for two months until Franco arrived with troops from North Africa.

The education system also promoted obedience to the regime. A textbook in the early years of the regime, which showed drawings of children giving the fascist salute, included the following: "He who takes responsibility must also take power. This is the reason why the state has all the power. Our sole duty as subordinates is to obey. We must obey without discussion. He who gives orders does so because he knows what he is doing."

What was the economic legacy of the Civil War?

The Civil War brought the economy, in which around half the labor force worked in agriculture, to its knees. The GDP declined 36 percent in real terms between 1935 and 1938. It was not until 1953 that the economic output recovered to its 1935 (pre–Civil War) level. The most pressing need was food. Rationing was introduced in 1939 and did not end until 1952. Many people tried to survive on grasses boiled in salted water. It is estimated that up to 200,000 Spaniards starved to death or died from diseases directly related to malnutrition between

1939 and 1945. Tuberculosis surged after the war. Argentina, one of Franco's very few allies, came to the rescue of the famine, one of Europe's least-known tragedies, with shipments of wheat and meat, but this did little to alleviate the suffering. The 1940s in Spain are still referred to today as *Los Años de Hambre* (The Years of Hunger). Per capita consumption of meat and wheat in 1950 was still just half the pre–Civil War level. The situation gave way to a flourishing black market. These lean years were depicted in the popular cartoon created by José Escobar in 1947 featuring Carpanta, a character who roasted his own shoe at the end of each strip's story.

The regime's economic policy was autarky (self-sufficiency), a natural ally of political authoritarianism and one that aggravated rather than resolved the problems. The cornerstone of this policy was import substitution. Spearheading the drive for industrial self-sufficiency was the Instituto Nacional de Industria (INI), a state holding company founded in 1941 and modeled on Mussolini's Istituto per la Ricostruzione Industriale. The INI provided centralized state initiatives for many sectors of industry, including coal, electricity, aluminum, aircraft, and shipbuilding. Private-sector activity was also heavily controlled, with both output and prices subject to regulation. This created shortages and produced companies unable to compete in international markets and so earn the foreign currency needed to import products for industrialization. Spain's exports in 1950s represented less than 4 percent of its GDP, the lowest level of all OECD countries except for Turkey. The system of import licenses, quotas, and permissions of all types was fertile ground for corruption. Autarky came to an end in 1959 (see the question below on the Stabilization Plan).

How was the Catholic Church rewarded for supporting General Franco?

The hierarchy of the church was quick to bless Franco's uprising against the Republic in 1936, calling it a crusade to restore

Christian values. One of Franco's very first actions in May 1939 after winning the war was to present the "sword of victory" to the Cardinal Archbishop of Toledo, Isidro Gomá y Tomás, who placed it in the cathedral of that city as "eloquent testimony of the faith of our Catholic people so worthily represented by their Caudillo in this culminating and transcendental moment of our nation." Given this symbiotic relationship, it was not surprising that the church became one of the pillars of the regime.

The renowned philosopher Miguel de Unamuno (1864–1936), rector of the University of Salamanca, clashed in a public confrontation with one of Franco's key generals, José Millán Astray, shortly after the war started. He prophetically announced, "You may conquer but you will never convince. This will be the victory of the worst, of a brand of Catholicism that is not Christian and of a paranoid militarism bred in the colonial campaigns." Millán Astray responded, "Death to intelligence! Long live death!" But for the intervention of Franco's wife, Unamuno would probably have been shot on the spot. He died a broken man.

The church's power and privileges, eroded during the Second Republic (1931–1939), were restored after Franco's victory and sealed in August 1953 by a concordat with the Vatican, which made Catholicism the state religion and granted the regime moral legitimacy. The close ties binding the civil and ecclesiastical powers were described as "National Catholicism." Religious instruction in all schools was compulsory, schools run by the church were subsidized, civil marriage was prohibited if either partner was a Catholic (Protestant religious marriages were illegal), priests were exempt from military service, and the state agreed to pay the clergy's salaries. Every classroom had a crucifix.

Bishops were members of the rubber-stamp Cortes (the parliament) and of the Council of the Realm (the highest advisory body), and members of the clergy also sat on censorship boards and held positions in the educational bureaucracy and in the syndicate (trade union) system. These advantages were the most generous enjoyed by the Spanish church since the days of absolute monarchy and made the church a kind of shadow government. Few churches in modern times have been more compromised.

Franco retained the right, conceded by the Vatican in 1941, to choose a bishop for a particular diocese from a short short-list previously agreed upon with the Holy See, from which, therefore, unsuitable names had already been excluded. Bishops swore allegiance to him in the following terms: "Before God and the Holy Gospels I swear and promise to respect, and cause to be respected by my clergy, the Head of the Spanish State and the Government issuing from the laws of Spain…Careful of the welfare and interests of the Spanish state, I will strive to avoid any evil that might threaten it."

The church held considerable sway over moral life and over what books people could read or films they could watch. In 1959, Enrique Plá y Deniel, the Cardinal Primate of Spain, declared that public bathing "constitutes a special danger for morality. Mixed bathing must be avoided because it almost always gives rise to sin and scandal. As for engaged couples, they must shun solitude and the dark. Walking arm in arm is unacceptable." The concordat was not substantially revised until 1979, by which point Spain was a parliamentary monarchy and a non-confessional state (see "What were the Socialists' relations with the Catholic Church"? in chapter 4).

Why was the 1953 military bases agreement with the United States important?

The US government of Harry Truman concluded at the end of the 1940s that its policy of isolating Spain had bolstered Franco, hindered the country's economic recovery, and made her cooperation less likely in the event of another world war. Dean Acheson, the secretary of state (1949–1953), said the policy had not only "failed in its intended purpose, but has served to strengthen the position of the present regime." With the Cold

War in full swing and Franco playing his staunchly anticommunist card as the "Sentinel of the West," the Pentagon eyed Spain as a place to establish military bases, given its geostrategic position. According to a secret report in 1947 by the Central Intelligence Agency, since declassified, "in the event of a war between the US and the USSR, the Iberian Peninsula, because of the Pyrenees, might serve as the site for a brief delaying action against a Soviet advance from France. The Peninsula's chief value to either belligerent, however, would be a site for air and naval bases from which to control the western Mediterranean and its Atlantic approaches."[3]

Spain was the US Strategic Air Command's missing link for closing its network of forward-deploying bases and encircling the Soviet Union. Other bases were established in Portugal's Azores in 1951 and in Turkey in 1952. The turning point came in June 1950 when Communist North Korea invaded South Korea, which had been under US control since the end of the Second World War. By then the Soviet Union had atomic bomb capability. Washington was also worried at the parlous state of the Spanish economy—"held together by baling wire and hope," according to a report by a US economic mission—and the potential for social unrest.[4] The anti-Communist witch hunt led by Senator Joe McCarthy also helped to create the appropriate atmosphere for a rapprochement with the regime. The US ambassador in Madrid had been withdrawn in 1946, and a new one took up the position in 1951.

Franco played hard to get and in return for bases held out for large amounts of aid, which Washington rejected. The Pact of Madrid to establish air bases at Torrejón (near Madrid), Sanjurjo de Valenzuela (near Zaragoza), and Morón de la Frontera (near Seville) and a naval base at Rota (near Gibraltar) was signed in 1953. Torrejón was the headquarters of the Sixteenth Airforce (16 AF) of the United States Air Forces in Europe (USAFE), as well as home to the 401st Tactical Fighter Wing (401 TFW). After signing the treaty, Franco is reported to have said, "Now I have won the Civil War."

The agreement was particularly controversial for the French and British governments, as they believed it undermined the moral authority of the Western bloc, while liberals in the United States, democrats in Spain, and Spaniards in exile viewed it as propping up the dictatorship. Instead of GIs liberating Spaniards from an authoritarian yoke, they consolidated the dictatorship and gave it a pervasive feeling of security. The accord, which was largely untouched until 1988, when the Socialist government renegotiated large parts of it, was a huge triumph for Franco, particularly as no political liberalization was demanded. It fostered a strong anti-US sentiment among the Spanish left that lasted until long after Franco's death in 1975.

The dictatorship gained international respectability and internally felt more secure with US troops on its soil. It also received around $625 million from the US government over six years. The naval base at Rota saved the US government tens of millions of dollars a year, as its submarines did not have to go to Charleston or New London every 56 days for replenishment and supply (a 14-day round-trip). Later, the runway at Rota became a valuable asset to the US Air Force when Washington lost its bases in Morocco in 1963. The runway was lengthened so that it could handle landings of B-52 bombers and KC-135 tankers in emergency situations. Rota became, and still is, one of the three largest and most important US bases outside continental America for strategic deterrence.

Spain was welcomed back into the Western fold, joining the United Nations in 1955, and the main institutions of capitalism—the International Monetary Fund, the World Bank, and the OEEC (the predecessor to the Organization for Economic Co-operation and Development, the OECD)—in 1959. But it was excluded from NATO until after Franco's death. President Dwight Eisenhower visited Spain in December 1959, but no European prime minister or head of state met Franco during his 39-year rule apart from the Portuguese dictator António de Oliveira Salazar.

What role did the 1959 Stabilization Plan play in creating a modern economy?

Twenty years of autarky (self-sufficiency), which did little to improve living standards, came to an end in 1959 shortly after Spain joined the International Monetary Fund (IMF). The Stabilization Plan, backed by the IMF and prepared by a group of prominent technocrats, several of whom were members of or close to Opus Dei, a predominantly lay and ultraconservative Catholic organization, was the first step in moving toward a market economy. In a memorandum to the IMF the technocrats said the "moment has arrived to change the economic policy in order to bring the Spanish economy into line with the countries of the West, and to free it from the policy of interventionism which, inherited from the past, is not appropriate to the needs of the present situation."

Multiple exchange rates were abolished, the peseta devalued, wages frozen, and some of the trade in private hands was liberalized. Restrictions on foreign direct investment were eased and economic policy became export-oriented. Between 1959 and 1974, real economic growth averaged 6.9 percent a year, a rate surpassed among developed nations only by Japan, albeit from a low base. The technocrats believed that economic prosperity would depoliticize Spain. "We shall start thinking about democracy when income per head of the population exceeds $1,000," said Laureano López Rodó, the chief architect of a series of development plans. (Per capita income at market prices crossed the $500 line in 1963 and $1,000 in 1971, four years before Franco died.) Franco admitted that without the reforms "we were heading towards bankruptcy." By 1960, when the current account was in surplus, the regime began to create a social security system, provide low-cost housing, expand education opportunities, create industries in chemicals, machinery, and shipbuilding, and manufacture consumer goods, including cars. The little Seat 600, built under license with Italy's Fiat, became as popular as the Mini in Britain. Car ownership increased from 4 percent of all households in 1960 to 35 percent in 1971.

Unemployment, however, remained high during the 1960s and forced people to emigrate. Between 1960 and 1973 it is estimated that 1.5 million Spaniards sought work in Germany, France, Switzerland, and other European countries. In 1970, 3.3 million Spaniards were estimated to be living abroad, the equivalent of one-quarter of the working population in Spain at that time. Luckily for Spain, the rest of Europe was expanding and the jobs provided abroad were a "safety valve" for a country that might otherwise have faced serious social unrest, particularly in rural areas, where more than one million people (10 percent of the working population) were underemployed and barely survived. Between 1959 and 1969, remittances from Spaniards working abroad amounted to $3.9 billion, higher than net foreign direct investment during this period.

Internal migration was also considerable. Between 1960 and 1970 more than three million people moved on a permanent basis within Spain—from villages and towns mainly to Madrid, Barcelona, and Bilbao, leading to the creation first of shanty districts on the outskirts of these cities and later the building of shoddy high-rise apartment blocks. Roughly speaking, more than one in every ten people changed their municipality of residence during this period. Migration within Spain from villages to towns and cities and emigration abroad changed social values, as it brought Spaniards into contact with more modern ways of life. The population in towns of less than 20,000 dropped from 71 percent of the total population in 1900 to 45 percent in 1979.

What is Opus Dei?

Opus Dei (the Work of God) was founded in 1928 by the Aragonese priest Josemaría Escrivá de Balaguer and is devoted to "finding God in daily life," a philosophy expressed in his book *Camino* (The Way). The book is a collection of 999 maxims, ranging from traditional Christian pieties such as "The prayer of a Christian is never a monologue" to sayings such as "Don't put off your work until tomorrow." Opus Dei is neither a religious order, like the Dominicans and the Jesuits, nor a secular institute or religious movement. It is a personal prelature, 95 percent of which is laity and only 5 percent clergy.

It was granted authority to practice in 1947 by Pope Pius XII. Today, there are more than 90,000 members spread around the world, many of whom occupy important positions in the state and the private sector. Opus Dei first came to prominence in Spain during the 1960s when technocrats who were members of or close to the organization drew up plans to modernize the economy and make it more competitive and efficient. At a time when Spain was an impoverished country, Opus Dei emphasized concepts such as productivity, competitiveness, and probity more than democracy. This led to its being criticized by democrats for being far too conservative and supportive of the Franco regime.

This was not the case, however, of all Opus Dei members. Rafael Calvo Serrer, a prominent member, founded the liberal newspaper *Madrid* in 1966. It was fined and banned on several occasions for its trenchant criticism of the regime and closed down in 1971. Over the years Opus Dei became increasingly influential in education, the judiciary, and banking and less so in government. The brightest students taking the *oposiciones*, the competitive exam to enter the civil service and the judiciary, were sometimes privately coached by Opus Dei members to ensure they did well and to win their loyalty. Pope John Paul II canonized Escrivá in 2002, calling him the "saint of ordinary life."

How did Spain become one of the world's main tourist destinations?

As part of a government restructuring in 1951, tourism was raised to a cabinet-level portfolio with the creation of a ministry. In 1959, the government abolished entry visas for tourists and devalued the peseta, making Spain even cheaper for visitors with hard currency. Spain also benefited greatly from the Europe-wide deregulation of package-tour air charters. The number of foreign visitors to Spain jumped 43 percent in 1960 to 4.3 million (more than France), 18 million in 1967, 30 million by 1975, and more than 57 million today (10 million more than its population), making it the world's fourth-largest tourism destination. Tourism became one of Spain's key industries, at 11 percent of its GDP.

Spain was blessed with hundreds of kilometers of virgin coastline that was quickly developed (and much of it eventually ravaged) with hotels and apartment blocks that were cheap by European standards. Benidorm, a sleepy village of fishermen and farmers on the Mediterranean coast in the 1960s, became the archetypal resort for the mass tourism and package tours that Spain is credited with pioneering. Today, Benidorm has Europe's tallest hotel, the Gran Bali, with 52 floors and 776 rooms. In addition to a plentiful supply of beaches, Spain has 44 UNESCO-declared World Heritage Sites, the most of any country after Italy.

The Franco regime marketed the country during the 1960s under the slogan "Spain is different," which was true in comparison to other European countries (that is, with the notable exceptions of the dictatorships in Portugal [1932–1974] and Greece [1967–1974]). Tourism, like the remittances from emigrants, provided much-needed hard currency and also played an important role in Spain's democratic development because it brought Spaniards into contact with different peoples and ideas, particularly from European democracies, and broadened their horizons. Paradoxically, tourism helped to make Spain a more "normal" country.

What was the opposition to the Franco regime?

Opposition to the regime took many different forms and was divided inside Spain and abroad. Broadly speaking, it was divided into *aperturistas* (those who advocated reform from within the regime) and *rupturistas* (those who wanted a complete break and full democracy). There were also divisions among monarchists. Alfonsine monarchists (named after Alfonso XIII, the last king of Spain, who went into exile in 1931 shortly before the Second Republic was proclaimed and who abdicated in 1941) backed Don Juan de Borbón, Alfonso XIII's son, while Carlist monarchists backed another dynasty.

Don Juan had secretly entered Spain in 1936 with the false identity of Juan López after the Civil War erupted and tried to join the Nationalist army, but he was put back over the French frontier. Franco later justified this action on the grounds that "if a King is again to be head of state, he should appear as a peacemaker and not come from the camp of the victors." In 1945, Don Juan called in his Lausanne Manifesto for an end to the "totalitarian" regime and a broad range of democratic freedoms. Although his relations with Franco were tense, Don Juan and Franco agreed at a meeting aboard the dictator's yacht, *Azor*, to let Don Juan's son, Juan Carlos, be educated in Spain as of 1948. This kept open the options of the Bourbon dynasty, which had ruled Spain for 250 years. Franco named Juan Carlos his successor in July 1969, against the wishes of his father, who felt that his position had been usurped (see "Who is King Juan Carlos?" in chapter 3). Don Juan lived most of his life in self-imposed exile in Portugal, from where he sniped at Franco and led a moderate opposition to the regime. His supporters were among the 80 delegates from Spain, together with 38 Republican exiles, who attended the meeting of the 4th Congress of the European Movement in Munich in June 1962. This was the first time Civil War victors and vanquished sat around the same table to discuss national reconciliation.

The congress adopted a resolution setting out the democratic reforms that had to be met before Spain could become a member of the European Economic Community (EEC). The government had submitted a request for membership to the EEC in February 1962. The regime furiously denounced the meeting as the *contubernio de Múnich* (the devious Munich Conspiracy). Those who returned to Spain were given the option of confinement in the Canary Islands for a year or imprisonment. One of those deported to the island of Fuerteventura, the Christian Democrat Fernando Álvarez de Miranda, became president of the Spanish parliament (1977–1979) after Franco died.

The Spanish Communist Party was by far the most organized and dedicated opposition force. In October 1944, after the French city of Toulouse had been liberated from the Nazis, a Communist force of several thousand guerrillas, many of whom had fought in the maquis (the resistance to the German occupation), crossed into northern Spain, where they were defeated by Franco's troops in the Valley of Aran. There was little support for them among a population struggling to survive. The Communists abandoned the armed struggle against the regime in 1948 and, after adopting a policy of national reconciliation in 1956, began to organize clandestinely inside Spain and infiltrate the trade unions, from where they pressed for better labor conditions. They also ran *Radio España Independiente* (Radio Free Spain) from Czechoslovakia, a station that could be heard in Spain. The sons and sometimes the daughters of the participants in the Civil War—and not just descendants of those from those on the losing side—were among those who worked clandestinely for the Communist Party. They sometimes shared a prison cell when they were arrested.[5] These common experiences played a part in the children of the victors and the vanquished, who were in leading positions in political and civic life at the end of the Franco regime, burying their differences and working together for democracy after the death of the dictator.

Most of the strikes and work stoppages in the 1962–1964 wave of protests were not politically motivated but related to pay and other issues. The regime cracked down on the strikers so harshly that it created political opposition. Organized dissent gathered strength in factories and in universities. Along with other opposition groups, the Communists set up the

Comisiones Obreras (CC OO, Workers' Commissions, today the main union), which were particularly effective in the metal industries in Madrid and Barcelona. In November 1962, Julián Grimau, a member of the Communist Party's central committee and its top underground agent in Spain, was arrested, tried by a military tribunal for killings he was accused of organizing during the Civil War (not for his illegal activities after the war was over), and executed by firing squad. This was the last death sentence for Civil War "crimes of blood."

The execution triggered massive protests abroad and in Spain, which the regime exploited to maintain the division between the victors and the vanquished and rally support. Jorge Semprún, a roving Communist agent based in Paris, used the same safe house in Madrid as Grimau.[6] Semprún went on to become a well-known novelist and screenwriter and culture minister (1988–1991) in the Socialist government of Felipe González. The Socialists were also forced to go underground after the Civil War but, compared to the Communists, played a relatively minor role in the opposition until Franco's death.

In November 1966, the regime's propaganda for the referendum on the new constitution or "organic law," which among other things gave Franco the right to appoint his heir, presented a "yes" vote as one for Spain and a "no" vote as one for Moscow. Ninety-six percent of voters ticked the "yes" box. The Communists renounced violence and gradually resigned themselves to not achieving any fundamental change until the death of Franco. At the same time, a revolutionary group called the ETA (the acronym in the Basque language for Basque Homeland and Freedom) emerged in the Basque Country in 1959 and sought an independent state by violent means.

The church, which had largely rallied around Franco's uprising in 1936, with the main exception of some Basque and Catalan priests loyal to a Republic that had granted their territories autonomy, began to rescind its support of the regime in the late 1950s. Christian Democrats formed two workers' organizations, the Hermandad Obrera de Acción Católica and the Juventud Obrera Católica. The regime tolerated them, as it did the Workers' Commissions initially. This perhaps occurred because the creation of the unions coincided with the church's new stand on human rights and its role in an increasingly secular and pluralistic society, expressed in the encyclicals Mater et Magistra (1961) and Pacem in Terris (1963) of Pope John XXIII, and in the Second Vatican Council (1962–1965). Franco had no desire to antagonize the Vatican.

By the 1960s around 40 percent of diocesan priests had not personally experienced the Civil War, while the elderly hierarchy had. The Second Vatican Council unleashed an intense debate in the Spanish church. The dissident Francoist Joaquín Ruiz Giménez, a former ambassador to the Vatican (1948–1951) and education minister (1951–1956), started the magazine *Cuadernos para el Diálogo* in 1963 along with left-wing Christian Democrat and Socialist intellectuals. The regime tolerated the magazine. Some liberal members of the clergy provided the sanctuary of parish houses, churches, and convents for opposition meetings. In 1963, Father Aureli María Escarré, abbot of the Benedictine monastery of Montserrat near Barcelona, gave an interview to the French newspaper *Le Monde*, which provoked the wrath of the regime and caused him to go into exile. "Spain is still divided into two parts," he said. "We have behind us not 25 years of peace, but merely 25 years of victory. The victors, the church included, have done nothing to put an end to the division into victors and vanquished. This is one of the most lamentable failures of a regime which calls itself Christian but in which the state does not obey the basic principles of Christianity."

In 1971, an assembly of bishops and priests voted on a resolution to apologize for the church's role in the Civil War, but it did not gain the two-thirds majority required for its adoption. By the end of the regime in 1975, relations between part of the church hierarchy and the dictatorship were acrimonious. Some priests were known as *curas obreros* (worker priests) because they identified with workers' movements close to or controlled by the Communist Party. The best-known "worker priest" was the Jesuit José María de Llanos, who was initially involved with the fascist Falange until he moved to a poor suburb of Madrid known as El Pozo del Río Raimundo. There was a special prison at Zamora for dissident clergy.

A survey conducted in the 1970s by the Foundation for the Development of Social Studies and Applied Sociology (FOESSA) among priests revealed that 69 percent disagreed with the social and political policies of the church hierarchy. On acceding to the archiepiscopal throne of Madrid in 1971, the liberal Cardinal Vicente Enrique y Tarancón (1907–1994), who was to play an important role during the transition to democracy, declared: "During several centuries a symbiosis has developed between the church and politics. This long phase is now at an end, and will be replaced by a phase of independence of the church in relation to the state." Tarancón, who was Spain's youngest bishop at the age of 39, became a bête noire of the extreme right: at the funeral in December 1973 of Franco's prime minister, Admiral Luis Carrero Blanco, assassinated by the ETA, he was harangued by Francoists to shouts of *Tarancón al paredón!* ("Tarancón to the firing squad!"). By distancing itself from the regime, the church prevented an anticlerical backlash after Franco died.

As the regime entered its twilight years, the opposition began to coalesce. First off the mark was the Communist Party, which formed a coalition in Paris in July 1974 called Junta Democrática (Democratic Junta) along with Izquierda Democrática (Democratic Left) of Ruiz Giménez, the Partido Socialista Popular (Popular Socialist Party, PSP) of Enrique Tierno Galvan (a university professor expelled from his post in 1965 in Salamanca after student protests), and a number of mavericks, including Carlos Hugo, the Carlist pretender to the Spanish throne. The mainstream Partido Socialista Obrero Español (Spanish Workers' Socialist Party), founded in 1879, refused to join, fearing the Communists would use it to gain respectability and hijack it for its own purposes. A year later, the Plataforma de Convergencia Democrática (Democratic

Convergence Platform) was established by the rest of the opposition, including the renovated Socialist Party under its new secretary-general, Felipe González. At the time, Gonzalez was a 33-year-old Andalusian lawyer living in Spain, who had replaced the historic exiled leader Rodolfo Llopis at the party's congress in Suresnes, France, in 1974. González went on to become prime minister between December 1982 and May 1996 (see "Who is Felipe González"? in chapter 4). Both groups sought a complete break with the regime, as they had concluded it was incapable of reforming itself.

What is the violent Basque separatist group ETA?

Two of the three Basque provinces—Vizcaya and Guipuzcoa—took the side of the Second Republic in the Civil War, while Alava generally supported General Franco and Navarra, which also spoke Basque, was the bastion of the ultra-Catholic Carlists. Vizcaya, Guipuzcoa, and Alava had a brief period of self-government until they fell into the hands of Franco's forces in June 1937, almost two years before the Civil War ended. Alava retained its historic privileges as a reward for helping Franco, as did Navarra. The towns of Durango and Guernica in the "traitor" province of Vizcaya were mercilessly bombed in April 1937 by German and Italian aircraft sent by Hitler and Mussolini, a tragedy immortalized in Pablo Picasso's mural-size painting *Guernica*, which he produced in Paris that same year and stipulated could not be seen in Spain until democratic liberties were restored. (The painting was shipped from New York's Museum of Modern Art to Madrid in September 1981, eight years after Picasso, who never returned to Spain, died, and is in the Reina Sofía museum. A tapestry copy hangs in the United Nations' headquarters in New York.) Among those executed by the advancing Nationalists were 14 Basque priests who supported the Republic.

After the Civil War the language and culture of the Basques, whose traditional guardians were the clergy, were suppressed.

In response, the Euskadi Ta Askatasuna (Basque Homeland and Freedom, ETA) was founded in 1959 by a group of young middle-class nationalists frustrated at the passivity of the Partido Nacionalista Vasco (PNV, Basque Nationalist Party), the historical party of Basque nationalism, most of whose leading members were in exile. The ETA's ideology was a mixture of traditional Basque nationalism, revolutionary socialism, and anticolonialism. Many of its first militants came from Catholic circles.

The group's goal was to create an independent Basque nation carved out of the four Spanish Basque provinces and three French ones on the other side of the Pyrenees. Its strategy was based on an approach known as "action-repression-action," which aimed to provoke the state into a spiral of repression after each of its actions. The group believed this would then trigger wider support for its cause and mobilize popular militancy against the dictatorship.

Its first large-scale operation was the botched derailing in 1961 of a train carrying Civil War veterans on Franco's side to San Sebastián to celebrate the 25th anniversary of the start of the war. The first ETA killing occurred in June 1968 when a car carrying ETA activists was stopped at a road check and in the ensuing gun battle a Civil Guard was shot. The first carefully planned assassination occurred that same year of Melitón Manzanas, the head of the *Brigada Politico-Social* (the political police) and a known torturer, in Irún on the Franco-Spanish border.

Basque nationalist hatred of the regime was epitomized in September 1970 when Joseba Elósegi, captain of a unit in Guernica when it was bombed on April 26, 1937, doused himself with petrol and set himself on fire. He did so during the world jai-alai championship (a ball game) in San Sebastián, which was presided over by Franco. He leaped from a height of 15 feet onto the court and landed near the dictator, shouting *Gora Euskadi Askatuta* ("Long Live a Free Basque Country!", a popular Basque slogan). He survived and was sentenced to seven years in prison.

In December 1970, 16 ETA members, including two priests, went on trial at Burgos, triggering demonstrations, strikes, and occupations of churches in support of the group and protests abroad. Six of the defendants were sentenced to death. Sentences of between 12 and 90 years were imposed on the others. Franco bowed to international pressure for clemency and commuted the death sentences to 30 years' imprisonment. He may also have been influenced by the preferential trade agreement Spain had signed with the European Economic Community a few months earlier.

The ETA's most spectacular single action came in December 1973, when it detonated a bomb in a T-shaped tunnel under the car of Admiral Luis Carrero Blanco, the prime minister and Franco's political heir. The blast hurtled his armored Dodge Dart, weighing more than two tons, 30 meters into the air and over the roof of the San Francisco de Borja Church in central Madrid, where he had just been attending mass. His assassination was in retaliation for the execution of two of the ETA's activists. He was the fifth head of government to be murdered in a little over a century. Spanish wits called Carrero Blanco the country's first astronaut. This was followed in September 1974 by a bomb attack in the Cafetería Rolando in Madrid, near to the police headquarters, which killed 13 people. Although self-government was restored in the Basque Country as of 1978, the ETA carried on assassinating for its cause of independence (see "Why did the ETA continue its violent campaign for an independent Basque state"? in chapter 3). Its single most brutal attack was in June 1987 when a bomb in a car park of a department store in Barcelona killed 21 people and injured 45. Of the 829 people killed by the ETA between 1959 and October 2011, when it announced a permanent cease-fire, only 45 were murdered during the Franco regime.

What impact did the ETA's assassination of Prime Minister Carrero Blanco in 1973 have on the regime?

The early 1970s were tumultuous years for Spain, with 817 strikes in 1970 alone. There were demonstrations calling for democracy and more killings by the Basque separatist group ETA, all of which caused the regime to crack down harshly on the group and opponents in general. None of this, however, deterred the tourism ministry from proclaiming in its slogan for 1971, "Feel free in Spain." At the age of 80, the ailing General Franco decided in June 1973 to separate the duties of chief of state and head of government and appoint Admiral Luis Carrero Blanco (aged 70) prime minister. A longtime confidant, Carrero Blanco had been deputy prime minister for the six preceding years and was seen as the person who would carry on the regime after Franco died. He was a monarchist, close to the conservative Catholic Opus Dei movement, whose technocrats had begun to liberalize the economy, and he knew the regime, from the many posts he had held, inside out. But he lasted only six months in the post, as he was assassinated on December 20, 1973, by the ETA. Many arrests were made after his killing, including that of Simón Sánchez Montero, one of the underground Communist leaders, but a state of emergency was not declared despite pressure from the extreme right.

Franco, devastated by the death of his closest colleague, appointed Carlos Arias Navarro, the hard-line interior minister and a former secret police chief, prime minister. He was known among the left as the "butcher of Malaga," as he had been a state prosecutor in that city after it fell to the Nationalists during the Civil War and a savage repression ensued. His appointment as the first civilian to head the government since 1939 coincided with the announcement on the very same day of more than usually harsh verdicts in the trial of the "Carabanchel Ten"—10 leaders of the illegal Workers' Commissions trade union. Marcelino Camacho was sentenced to 20 years' imprisonment and the Jesuit Father Francisco García Salve, a worker priest, 19 years.

Despite being a fervent Francoist, Arias promised a political opening in a speech to the Cortes (parliament) on February 12, 1974, but his words were hollow. Political associations (not parties, a word banned from the regime's lexicon) would be allowed—but only provided they were compatible with the National Movement, the only legal political organization. Twelve days later, relations between the regime and the church plunged into crisis when Monsignor Antonio Añoveros Ataún, the bishop of Bilbao, published a pastoral letter requesting the recognition of Basque cultural and linguistic identity. This was a taboo subject and provoked the wrath of the state. Añoveros was placed under house arrest and refused to resign his post and leave Spain unless Pope Paul VI asked him to go. After the pope threatened to excommunicate Arias if the bishop was expelled, the regime relented.

The next blow came from the peaceful overthrow on April 25, 1974, of the 40-year dictatorship in neighboring Portugal, which Spaniards were able to watch on television. This event entrenched the dictatorship, as did the toppling of the Greek military junta that July. General Manuel Díez-Alegria, the relatively liberal chief of the Spanish army staff, was dismissed after he visited Rumania and met Santiago Carrillo, the exiled leader of the Communist Party. Diéz-Alegria was viewed as someone who might play the role that General António de Spinola had played in Portugal's military coup against the dictatorship. It was said that he was sent monocles anonymously (Spinola wore one). This was a symbolic way of asking him to intervene.

Caught between the pressure to reform and the wrath of ultra-Francoists known collectively as "the Bunker," Arias sided with the Francoists. Unlike at the 1973 Burgos trial of Basque separatists belonging to the ETA, the regime showed no mercy at the trial on September 27, 1975, of five militants accused of killing three policemen. They were shot by firing squad under a draconian antiterrorist law that made death sentences obligatory. A group of prominent French figures, including the actor Yves Montand and the writer Regis Debray, were expelled from Madrid after they tried to hold a press conference to protest the death sentences. Plainclothes policemen escorted some of the journalists, including me, to police headquarters for questioning. The execution of two members of the ETA and three members of the Maoist Revolutionary Antifascist Patriotic Front (FRAP) triggered strikes in Spain, protests abroad, the recalling of ambassadors from eight European Economic Community (EEC) countries, and the suspension of trade talks with the EEC. The five were among the more than 300 civilians who appeared before military courts in 1974–1975 for various crimes. The regime responded with a 150,000-strong rally of support for Franco, who appeared on the balcony of the royal palace in Madrid with Prince Juan Carlos, his designated heir, where he denounced the "Masonic leftist conspiracy of the political class in collusion with communist-terrorist subversion." It was his last public appearance. On October 30 Franco suffered a heart attack, and he died on November 20. His dictatorship was the only one in 20th-century Europe outside the Communist countries not to be violently overthrown.[7]

How much did the economy and society change during the Franco regime?

Between 1960 and 1975, Spain's economic and social change and wealth creation was profound and took place over a much shorter period of time than in other European countries (see table 2.1). The society that Franco left when he died bore no resemblance to that which existed before his uprising in 1936. The changes brought stability and reduced the regime's need for repression to maintain itself in power. Yet the political structures remained ossified and out of sync with the country's profound transformation.

The "economic miracle," as of the 1960s, created a much larger middle class (33 percent of the total population in 1970 compared to 14 percent in 1950) and rid Spain of the huge gulf between rich and poor that existed before the Civil War. Agriculture's share of the GDP dropped from 24 percent

Table 2.1 Basic Socioeconomic Statistics, 1960–1975

	1960	1975
Population (million)	30.9	36.0
Per capita income ($)	248	3,186
Structure of gross domestic product (%)		
Agriculture	27	9.0
Industry	30	39.0
Services	43	52.0
Employment by sector (% of the active population)		
Agriculture	44	21.8
Industry	24	37.8
Services	32	40.4
Export earnings ($million)	725	6,583
Structure of exports (% of total)		
Agriculture	56	23
Industrial goods	33	60
Raw materials	11	8
Tourists (million)	6	30
Emigrants' remittances ($million)	57	700
Net foreign direct investment ($million)	123	430
Cost of living (index)	100	375
Earnings (index)	100	1,000
Telephones per 1,000 population	56	210
TV sets per 1,000 population	5	190
Cars per 1,000 population	10	125
Car production	39,600	696,000
Tractors in use	71,000	336,700
Donkeys and mules	1,850,000	570,000
Steel production (million tons)	1.9	11.1
Cement production (million tons)	5.2	23.9
Dwellings built (mainly apartments)	127,800	374,200

Source: The Economist. Compiled from the magazine's survey of Spain published on April 2, 1977.

to 9 percent between 1960 and 1975 as the economy became more industrial and services-based. The proportion of the population living in towns and cities rose from 46 percent to 55 percent, and the number of cities with more than 100,000 inhabitants increased from 26 to 38. Per capita income in 1975 was $2,865, creating a consumer society. The number of cars per 1,000 people increased from 10 in 1960 to 125 in 1975.

Many workers could afford to take their first holidays by the sea in the 1960s when the country's tourism industry was burgeoning. The greater prosperity enabled the state to invest significantly in roads, railways, bridges, tunnels, and reservoirs. In a country prone to drought, water-storage capacity increased sixfold. Spending on education also rose. The primary school enrollment rate more than doubled to 88.3 percent between 1960 and 1970, and the rate of illiteracy dropped from 13.7 percent to 8.8 percent.

Women's position in society also advanced considerably, despite the traditional role assigned to them. Women accounted for 30 percent of the workforce in 1974, double the number in 1950. Society was also increasingly secular and less influenced by the Catholic Church, a pillar of the regime until its last years.

The press, though not other parts of the media, became freer as a result of a law in 1966 that did away with prior censorship by the state and replaced it with self-censorship on the part of editors. It was far from a liberal law, but it gave newspapers such as the relatively liberal *Informaciones* and magazines such as the humorous *La Codorniz* and the progressive *Triunfo* greater freedom and also led to the launch of new publications like *Cambio 16*, although some issues were confiscated for overstepping the limits. The arts were also freer. The main filmmakers were Carlos Saura (*La Prima Angélica*, My Cousin Angélica), Víctor Erice (*El Espíritu de la Colmena*, The Spirit of the Beehive), Basilio Martín Patino (*Canciones para después de una Guerra*, Songs for after a War), and in literature the most influential figures were the poet Vicente Alexaindre and the novelists Camilo José Cela (*La Colmena*, The Hive) and Miguel Delibes (*El Camino*, The Path). Alexaindre and Cela were Nobel laureates in 1977 and 1989, respectively. There were also protest singer-songwriters such as Joan Manuel Serrat, Raimón, and Paco Ibáñez. Spaniards were no longer fed a constant stream of eulogies of the regime, and books, even some Marxist ones, were more readily available. George Orwell's *Homage to Catalonia*, his book about his experiences on the Republican side during the Civil War, was published in 1970 with only one passage deleted. Some bookshops selling such books were attacked by the Guerrilleros del Cristo Rey (Warriors of Christ the King), an ultra-right-wing group.

Opinion polls in the 1970s showed Spaniards were increasingly overcoming the divisions caused by the Civil War, paving the way for reconciliation. According to a survey in 1975, 74 percent of respondents wanted press freedom, 71 percent religious freedom, and 58 percent trade union freedom. These socioeconomic changes, however, did not automatically guarantee a successful transition to democracy after Franco died. The international context was also very different. Spain was firmly anchored in the Western bloc, as a result of the 1953 agreement allowing the United States to establish military bases in the country. It also had a preferential trade agreement as of 1970 with the European Economic Community, the club of European democracies that the dictatorship had been rejected from in 1962.

3

THE TRANSITION TO DEMOCRACY, 1975–1982

What happened when Franco died?

Franco, the chief protagonist of nearly half a century of Spanish history, died on November 20, 1975, at the age of 82. He was wired and plugged into a battery of medical machines, with the arm of Saint Teresa beside him and the mantle of the Virgin of the Pillar, Spain's female patron saint, on his bed. Tens of thousands of Spaniards queued to see the dictator as he lay in state; some joked that they did so in order to ensure that he really was dead. The majority of the population had never known another political system. The 37-year-old Prince Juan Carlos had taken over as head of state three weeks earlier as Franco had named him his successor over the prince's father, Don Juan de Borbón, the pretender to the Spanish throne, whom the dictator regarded as a liberal.

In his first address to the parliament, Juan Carlos made it clear he wanted to be the "king of all Spaniards, without exception," an oblique reference to his desire for national reconciliation. Franco had left his regime and its institutions "tied up and well tied up," and it now fell to Juan Carlos to unravel the knots so that democracy could be restored. The king and his circles were acutely aware that to break with the regime too quickly might provoke a military coup and that to go too slowly would unleash the pent-up frustration of Spaniards impatient for democratic change and ready for it as a result of economic and social change. Either way, the monarchy, the only institution that was not identified with either side in the Civil War, and therefore the only one that could move the country forward, was at risk.

The king's limited general pardon, issued less than a week after Franco died, did not benefit many of the 2,000 political prisoners, although the most famous one, Marcelino Camacho, a well-known trade unionist, was released from Carabanchel Prison in Madrid after serving three and a half years of a six-year sentence. He had been convicted of leading the Comisiones Obreras (CC OO, Workers' Commissions), an illegal Communist-controlled trade union. He had spent a total of 14 years in prison. Another immediate consequence of Franco's death was the showing in cinemas of Charlie Chaplin's film *The Great Dictator*, 35 years after it was first released, and other banned films such as *Last Tango in Paris*. Spaniards flocked over the French border to see this film when it was released in 1972. It was seen in Perpignan, for example, by 110,000 viewers, while the town's population numbered only around 100,000.

The king kept the recalcitrant Francoist Carlos Arias Navarro, who had wept when he announced the dictator's death on television, as prime minister. The king also kept the three military ministers. He balanced this by appointing relatively liberal politicians to the Cabinet, including José María de Areilza as foreign minister. He also reshuffled familiar figures, many of them former ministers under Franco, including the authoritarian Manuel Fraga, who saw himself as leading a European-style conservative party, as prime minister. Arias's promise to change laws as "Franco would have wished" dismayed the reformist right and lost him what little credibility he had with the left, which mobilized massive demonstrations for an amnesty for political prisoners and exiles and the recognition of all political parties. Bishops also added their voices to the amnesty demand. Extreme-right groups, such as Fuerza Nueva (New Force), took to the streets in much smaller numbers to defend the regime and condemn democracy. The mandate of members of Franco's last parliament was prolonged for a year to allow time to move the country along the road to democracy, but progress was very slow.

The government's timid course of liberalization exposed the profound contradictions in the cabinet between the inflexible old guard (collectively known as "the Bunker") and the handful of reformist ministers. In the Basque Country, for example, the nationalist flag was unfurled in December 1975 for the first time in public in 36 years without police intervention, while demonstrators calling for an amnesty were baton charged and arrested. In March 1976, a group of army officers who had formed the illegal Democratic Military Union were put on trial and imprisoned for between two and eight years. In another trial nine Communists were jailed for belonging to an illegal organization. The press was also intimidated, and torture of some political detainees continued. The magazine *Cuadernos para el Diálogo* withdrew a report on torture by the Civil Guard and the secret police after the editor was told the issue would be seized and he would be called to testify before a military court.

In this tense environment, the main left-wing opposition groups put aside their differences and formed an alliance called Democratic Coordination, also known as the *Platajunta*. It was the joint product of the Communist-founded Democratic Junta and the socialist-based Platform of Democratic Convergence, which pressed for a faster pace of democratic reforms. The left's chronic factionalism was one of the factors that plagued the Republic. The king, caught between the immovable Bunker and a left that was flexing its muscles, became increasingly impatient with Arias and in July provoked his resignation by telling the US magazine *Newsweek* that his prime minister was an "unmitigated disaster."

Who is King Juan Carlos?

Juan Carlos Víctor María de Borbón y Borbón was born in Rome in 1938 in the middle of the Spanish Civil War. The royal family had by then been seven years in exile after Juan Carlos's grandfather, Alfonso XIII, left Spain on the eve of the proclamation of the Second Republic in 1931. Alfonso abdicated in favor of Juan Carlos's father, Don Juan, in 1941, six weeks before he died.

After the Civil War, in 1945, Don Juan called for General Franco to "recognize the failure of the totalitarian conception of the state" and to restore the monarchy. Franco ignored the call and snubbed Don Juan in the 1947 referendum when Spain was declared a "Catholic, social and representative monarchy," with Franco as the lifetime uncrowned monarch with the right to name his successor. Despite the deep rift, the two of them agreed that year to send Juan Carlos to Spain to be educated. Franco did not want to alienate the monarchy, which he wanted to use for his own ends and upon whom he relied to some extent for support, while Don Juan wished to leave the door open so that one day the monarchy might return under him or his son.

Juan Carlos was only 10 when he traveled from Lisbon to Madrid (the family was then living at nearby Estoril) and became over the years a pawn in the dispute between his father and the dictator. He was a sad-looking child, separated for long periods at a time from his parents and drawn into the cold bosom of Franco, who never had a son. His younger brother, Alfonso, died at the age of 14, while the two of them were playing with a loaded gun. Juan Carlos had a formidable team of private tutors and was set a rigorous schedule, beginning with mass before breakfast. After his secondary education, he attended the army, air force, and navy academies, where he gained many contacts that would prove to be useful during the transition to democracy. Franco liked to give him history lessons in what he saw as the errors made by various ancestors of Juan Carlos's.

In 1960, Juan Carlos married Sofia, the daughter of King Paul of Greece and brother of Constantine. Constantine succeeded his father in 1964 and was forced to flee the country in 1967 after a military coup that led to the abolition of the monarchy. In 1969, Franco named Juan Carlos the next head of state, causing him to be estranged from his father. Juan Carlos was so affected by the nomination and egged on by various Francoists to confront his father to abdicate that thinking about it made him cry. Juan Carlos realized that to have rejected the succession in favor of his father would probably have cost both of them the crown. This was because there was a risk at the time that the dictator would name Juan Carlos's cousin, Alfonso, as his successor. Alfonso later married Franco's granddaughter Carmen in 1971, after Juan Carlos's nomination. (Alfonso's father, Don Jaime, born deaf and dumb, had renounced his claim to the throne in favor of his younger brother, Don Juan.) Juan Carlos accepted the nomination in the only terms that he could by swearing allegiance to the regime and to the "political legitimacy which rose from July 18, 1936," the date of Franco's uprising against the Republic.

Juan Carlos's public statements were vague and vacuous, as they could only be. In private, however, Juan Carlos made it clear to those he trusted that he intended to be the symbol of reconciliation and restore democracy. As Franco's heir, he realized that firm support for democracy was the only way to gain legitimacy and win backing for the monarchy. The Communist leader Santiago Carrillo dubbed him "Juan Carlos the Brief" in the belief that as Franco's puppet his reign would be short lived.

A few months before Franco died, in November 1975, Don Juan was banned from setting foot in Spain after he said his son's nomination was "logically no use at all in bringing democratic change." Unlike his father, Juan Carlos believed democratization could be accomplished from inside the regime. The king's academic and military education had given him an intimate understanding of how the regime functioned and how it could be changed from within. History indicates that transitions from dictatorship to democracy tend to be more stable and have a better chance of succeeding if they are engineered from above by elites from within the outgoing regime rather than from below. Juan Carlos maintained the reactionary Carlos Arias Navarro as prime minister in the first post-Franco government, which lasted only eight months, while actively encouraging the democratic forces. A total and sudden break with the regime was not possible as this would have deprived Juan Carlos of the only authority he enjoyed, which came from Francoist legislation. It might also have triggered a coup from those in the armed forces aligned against democracy, but they were loyal and obedient to the new head of state because he had been appointed by Franco.

The king bided his time and in July 1976 replaced Arias with Adolfo Suárez, the man chosen to unravel the regime. As the march to democracy finally began to progress, Juan Carlos, more astute than he was given credit for, was hailed as the "pilot" of change and no longer called "Juan Carlos the Brief." Carrillo said that but for the king, "the shooting would have already begun."

In May 1977, shortly before the first democratic election in 41 years, Don Juan renounced his rights to the throne so that in the drafting of the new constitution the democratic parliament would face no question as to who was king. The constitution consolidated the monarchy and Juan Carlos secured it on February 23, 1981, when, as head of the armed forces and in full military regalia, he went on television to face down a coup staged by a nostalgic minority who aimed at turning back the clock. Juan Carlos ordered the perpetrators to surrender (see "Why was there an attempted coup in 1981?" below).

The monarchy is popular in Spain. According to an opinion poll conducted on the 80th anniversary of the proclamation of the Second Republic in 1931, 48 percent of respondents said the monarchy was a better political system than a republic, compared to 39 percent who preferred a republic. Several embarrassing incidents since then, however, tarnished the royal family's image and prestige. The World Wildlife Fund removed the king as its honorary president in 2012 for going on an elephant-hunting trip in Botswana, and his son-in-law, Iñaki Urdangarin, was under investigation for alleged fraud, tax evasion, and embezzlement of public funds related to Nóos, the non-profit foundation he ran. The king's pricey African safari during a time of national hardship led him to publicly apologize and make the royal household's annual budget more transparent. At the end of 2012, 53 percent of respondents in a survey conducted by Metroscopia expressed support for a parliamentary monarchy as the best system for Spain compared to 72 percent in 1998. Over the same period, support for the restoration of a republic increased from 11 percent to 37 percent.

How was the transition to democracy achieved?

The transition to democracy began in earnest with the resignation of Prime Minister Carlos Arias Navarro in July 1976 and his replacement by the much younger Adolfo Suárez, a former head of the state-run television channel (TVE) and minister of the National Movement, the only legal political organization in Arias's government. Suárez was from the same generation as the king (both of them were born during the 1930s) but was not tainted by the Civil War. His appointment initially delighted Francoists and horrified the opposition until it became clear that, unlike Arias, Suárez was serious about reform. His promotion was stage-managed by Torcuato Fernández Miranda, the private law tutor of King Juan Carlos and head of the Cortes (parliament) and of the Consejo del Reino (Council of the Realm), the highest advisory body and the one responsible for selecting three people from which the king would choose the prime minister. Fernández Miranda slipped Suárez's name onto the list almost unnoticed; he was regarded as having no chance of getting the job. In fact, it was all part of a carefully crafted maneuver to use Francoist "legality" and a National Movement apparatchik to achieve democracy gradually rather than by engineering a swift break with the regime, which would have run the risk of provoking the old guard.

The transition was facilitated by a bureaucracy that was able to distinguish between service to the state and service to a particular government. Thus it did not require a prior or simultaneous transformation before the regime could move to democracy. Furthermore, as Franco's regime was a dictatorship of a military man rather than a military dictatorship, at the time of his death it was not necessary to dislodge the military from power. With the exception of those at either end of the political extremes, there was no desire to open up the divisions caused by the Civil War. The left realized that its push for a provisional government and a constituent parliament to decide on the form of regime was utopian and that it would have to negotiate patiently with the regime's reformists. Consensus, after so polarized a past, was very much the watchword between the reformist right and the nonviolent left. This was epitomized by the *Pacto de Olvido* (literally, Pact of Forgetting), an unspoken agreement among political elites to look ahead and not rake over the past. Looking backward could have destabilized the transition, as happened in Argentina after military trials got under way. The pact was institutionalized by the 1977 Amnesty Law.

The big difference between Spain and other dictatorships that moved to democracy in the 20th century was that the Spanish one was born out of a devastating civil war. None of the parties had any interest in having the role they played during the Second Republic before the Civil War put under the microscope, as this would have opened a Pandora's box of potentially violent consequences. There was nothing resembling a Truth and Reconciliation Commission along the lines of the one Chile set up shortly after the end of the Pinochet dictatorship in 1990. At the grassroots and local levels, however, the amnesty law did not prevent the early opening of mass graves of Republican supporters executed during and after the Civil War, nor the payment of pensions to former Republican military and police officers. Likewise, it could not stem the publication of many memoirs and novels and serious historical research on the war and its aftermath.

The opposition's stance toward the transition was summed up by Enrique Tierno Galvan, a Socialist professor and later a very popular mayor of Madrid. "If the government wants to construct a house [democratic Spain], furnish it and then invite us in it as tenants, then negotiation is not going to be possible. If, on the other hand, it invites the opposition to construct the house and furnish it, then negotiation is possible." The latter is what happened: in sharp contrast to the Franco regime, an inclusive political system was established.

Suárez was greatly aided by General Manuel Gutiérrez Mellado, the chief of the General Staff, who replaced the staunchly Francoist General Fernando de Santiago y Díaz de Mendívil as Suárez's deputy prime minister for defense when de Santiago resigned in September 1976, over a disagreement with the government's plan to abolish the Francoist trade union structure and allow free unions. De Santiago protested that the unions were "responsible for the outrages committed in the red zone (the area held by the Republicans in the Civil War)." Gutiérrez Mellado said he was a liberal "if you mean that I am opposed to fratricidal strife and that I believe Spain should belong to all Spaniards." He abolished the army, air force, and navy ministries and combined them in a new defense ministry, which he headed. He also tried to change the mind-set of officers, particularly those who had fought in the Civil War on Franco's side. He retired the most Francoist ones and replaced them with moderate officers. The general made the changes at great personal risk. He was regularly insulted and harassed by hard-line officers.

Parliament approved the reform of the penal code, permitting political activity for the first time in 37 years except by the Communists, the most organized force, which remained banned under pressure from Francoist diehards. The king decreed a partial amnesty for political prisoners and exiles, but not for those convicted of crimes of blood, leaving 145 members of the Basque separatist group ETA in prison. Various people were also barred from returning to Spain, including the 82-year-old

Dolores Ibárruri, the legendary Communist leader known as La Pasionaria, who was famous for her use of the expression "they shall not pass" (referring to Franco's troops) during the Civil War. The continued ban on the Communists dented the credibility of the general election promised for 1977. Santiago Carrillo, the party's exiled and veteran secretary-general, challenged the government's sincerity by crossing into Spain from France wearing a wig so that he would not be recognized by police at the border. He was arrested in Madrid and imprisoned in December 1976, shortly after the Francoist parliament approved the political reform law, thereby voting itself out of office. This paved the way for parliamentary democracy and a constitutional monarchy. Only 59 hard-core members of Franco's last parliament voted against the reforms; the 425 who amazingly voted in favor did so out of a mixture of obedience to authority, patriotism, and in some cases the promise of seats in the new senate. Voter turnout in the December 15, 1976, referendum on political reform was 78 percent, with 97 percent of voters supporting the reforms despite a boycott campaign waged by the left. The Public Order Court for political offenses was then abolished, enabling Carrillo to be freed after a week in prison and the Communist Party to be legalized on April 9, 1977, a week after the National Movement ended. Not to have authorized the party would have given the Communists an importance they did not have. Carrillo had agreed in secret negotiations with Suárez to recognize the monarchy and the unity of Spain and cooperate in dealing with the economic crisis, as it controlled the Comisiones Obreras (CC OO, Workers' Commissions), the main trade union. The Communist Party wanted to burnish its respectability. It was very disciplined and pragmatic; when four of its lawyers were murdered by ultra-right-wing terrorists, as part of a strategy of tension to derail the moves toward democracy, the leadership refused to be provoked and staged a massive silent march through Madrid. The party's legalization outraged reactionary officers in the armed forces and provoked the resignation of Admiral

Gabriel Pita de Veiga, the navy minister. According to secret reports by the intelligence services of the armed forces, most officers above the rank of lieutenant colonel were opposed to the legalization of the Communists.

Spain held its first free general election since February 1936 (five months before Franco's military uprising) on June 15, 1977. A veritable alphabet soup of 70 political parties and 4,537 candidates ran for the 350-member parliament. The political situation in the village where I have a house mirrored that of the countryside as a whole. With very few telephones and the nearest place to buy newspapers 17 km away, villagers' only link with the outside world was the state-run television. The secretary of the village's town hall, a Francoist, was the first to place his vote in the 100-year-old urn that held the ballots, so he could show the three election officials how the system worked. This was the first time that most of the electorate of the village (391 people) had voted in an election.

The Unión del Centro Democrático (UCD, the Union of the Democratic Center), a loose and hastily formed coalition of 12 groups, including the more progressive segments of the Francoist bureaucracy—liberals, Christian Democrats, and social democrats headed by Suárez—won 34.4 percent of the vote and 166 of the 350 seats. The Partido Socialista Obrero Español (PSOE, the Spanish Workers' Socialist Party), led by Felipe González, won 29.3 percent and 118 seats; the Partido Comunista Español (PCE, Spanish Communist Party), led by Carrillo, won 9.3 percent and 20 seats; and the neo-Francoist Alianza Popular (AP, Popular Alliance) of Manuel Fraga, a former information and tourism minister under the dictator and an authoritarian interior minister in the first government after Franco's death, obtained 8.2 percent and 16 seats. Fraga was seriously mistaken in his belief that the dictatorship had made a large part of the electorate conservative. The other 31 seats went to Catalan, Basque, and six other parties. Voter turnout was almost 80 percent. Franco's most ardent supporters, despite not believing in political parties, fielded several of them in the election and between them gained less than 1 percent of the total vote.

The results were a victory for the reformist right over the neo-Francoist right and for the moderate left over the radical left and clearly expressed Spaniards' desire to turn the page on the dictatorship. The UCD's victory prevented a polarization between the extremes of left and right, which would have been a dangerous climax to a transition period. The church's hierarchy in Spain also played a positive role by not using its considerable influence and power to openly back a Christian Democrat Party, as it did during the Second Republic (1931–1936), when it supported the CEDA. As a predominantly Catholic country, Spain was fertile soil for such a party along the lines of Germany and Italy, although the Christian Democrat movement in the country was very divided. Cardinal Vicente Enrique y Tarancón, the archbishop of Madrid and head of the Episcopal Conference (the bishops' organization), feared that a confessional party would revive the anticlericalism that beset the Republic and was one factor that led to the uprising of General Franco that sparked the Civil War.

La Pasionaria, in a symbolic act of reconciliation, presided over the inaugural meeting of the new parliament, and the king referred to himself for the first time in public as a "constitutional monarch." The last time La Pasionaria had spoken in parliament was in 1936, when the country was on the brink of civil war. The first law approved by the new parliament in October 1977 granted an amnesty for those who had not benefited from the amnesty in 1976, including for crimes of bloodshed, and stipulated that political crimes committed before December of that year could not be prosecuted. This drew a line under the dictatorship and granted impunity. Since then, this law has been invoked to dismiss investigations into Franco-era crimes for which there were no Truth and Reconciliation Commissions or Depuration Committees along the lines of those introduced in countries like Chile, South Africa, and Uruguay (see the question in chapter 6 on the Law of Historical Memory).

Who is Adolfo Suárez?

Adolfo Suárez, the politician chosen by King Juan Carlos to dismantle the Franco regime, was born in Cebreros, a village in the province of Avila, in 1932, one year after the Second Republic was established and four years before the start of the Civil War. His father was a government lawyer and he, too, took a law degree. Strikingly handsome, Suárez came to the notice of Fernando Herrero Tejador, the civil governor and provincial head of the National Movement, the only legal political organization in Avila, a province with a reputation for being conservative and staunchly Catholic. Suárez held various posts in the Movement, which was the only way for ambitious young men to advance politically. He became a member of Franco's rubber-stamp parliament at the age of 35, and civil governor of Segovia and provincial head of the Movement a year later. He came to the attention of the king between 1969 and 1973, when he was head of the state-run television, where he promoted the image of Juan Carlos and reportedly told him how the regime could be changed from within. In 1975, he was second in command of the Movement at the national level and head of it, with cabinet rank, in the first post-Franco government of the hard-line Carlos Arias Navarro at the end of that year. Also that year, he was one of the first of the regime's bureaucrats to take advantage of the law allowing political associations within the principles of the Movement, when he formed the Union of the Spanish People.

The knowledge, experience, and contacts that Suárez gained, coupled with the fact that he was not clearly identified with any of the currents of Francoism or associated with any of the regime's scandals, put him in an ideal position to reform the regime from within when the king got rid of Arias. The main political hurdle he faced was the legalization of the Communist Party. Although he had been a loyal servant of the Franco regime, and hence part of a caste that was generally out of touch with the extent to which society had changed during 36 years of one-party rule, Suárez had well-developed political antennae. This led him to declare, in one of his celebrated phrases, that "it is necessary to make politically real what is already real in the streets." Opinion polls showed there was wide support for legalizing the Communists. Suárez won the backing of the top military brass on the topic of the legalization of political parties by telling them the Communist Party would be excluded. At the same time, he was engaging in long and secret negotiations with Santiago Carrillo, the party's leader, to allow the party to return in exchange for not rocking the monarchist boat. The party was legalized during Easter of 1977 when many Spaniards, including major figures in the armed forces, were on holiday. When outraged generals accused him of deceit, he said his promise had been superseded by events, as he had won concessions from the Communists.

The legalization of all political parties cleared the last hurdle for the general election in June 1977, the first free one in 41 years. Suárez needed a party to contest the election and maneuvered himself into a position as the leader of a centrist coalition of 12 groups, the Unión del Centro Democrático (UCD, Union of the Democratic Center), formed less than two months before Spaniards went to the polls. It was a catchall alliance held together by personal ambition for power and not a common ideology. Some of the groups were so small that Spaniards joked at the time that all their members could fit into a taxi. The UCD's contradictions and infighting led to its imploding and virtually disappearing from the political scene as of the 1982 election, which Suárez contested as the head of a new party, the Centro Democrático y Social (CDS, Democratic and Social Center). The CDS won only two seats and 2.9 percent of the vote.

How important was grassroots mobilization and strike action in pressuring the regime to change?

The transition to democracy was crafted from the top by King Juan Carlos and elite pacts between the reformist right and the left. However, there was intense bottom-up pressure for change, manifested through massive demonstrations and strikes in favor of an amnesty for political prisoners, the legalization of political parties and trade unions, and regional autonomy.

Thousands of grassroots associations emerged after the end of the dictatorship. The main trade unions in the years before the Civil War were the Unión General de Trabajadores (UGT, General Union of Workers), founded in 1888 and historically affiliated with the Partido Socialista Obrero Español (PSOE, the Spanish Workers' Socialist Party), and the anarchist Confederación Nacional del Trabajo (CNT, National Confederation of Labor), established in 1910. The Franco regime had outlawed both, conveying the only legal authority to represent workers (and employers) on the official *sindicatos* (syndicates).

The Communist Party began to infiltrate trade unions during the 1960s and set up a parallel organization known as the Comisiones Obreras (CC OO, Workers' Commissions). They enjoyed semilegal existence as they represented workers' interests better than the syndicates and were often the only means for resolving labor disputes, but were finally outlawed in 1969. Marcelino Camacho, a member of the Communist Party's central committee and the best-known leader of the CC OO during the dictatorship, spent a total of 14 years in prison, and after the death of General Franco in November 1975 became the first general secretary of the CC OO.

In the first six months of 1976, as the government of Carlos Arias Navarro dragged its feet over reform, Spain was rocked by a wave of strikes and sit-ins calling for democratic change and not just for better wages and working conditions. Trade unions were legalized in April 1977. Workers were particularly militant in the Basque Country and staged strikes and demonstrations after policemen fatally shot protesters and tortured suspected members of the violent Basque separatist group ETA. Nearly 17 million workdays were "lost" because of strike activity during 1977, compared to less than two million per year in the last years of the dictatorship.

What role did the Spanish media play in the transition to democracy?

In the twilight years of the regime, new weekly magazines appeared such as *Cambio 16*, *Doblón*, and *Triunfo*, all of which showed increasing boldness, even at the risk of fines and seizure of issues. When Franco died in November 1975 they and other publications constituted a kind of shadow government constantly calling for amnesty, democratic reforms, and, most important of all, a general election.

Some journalists were attacked for going about their business. José Antonio Martínez Soler, editor of *Doblón*, was seized in February 1976 and driven into the country, where, bound and blindfolded, he was beaten on the head and soles of his feet. His crime was to have published a mild article about the Civil Guard in which he said that some were members of the banned Democratic Military Union. His kidnappers wanted a list citing names. But for the fact that he managed to break free after his kidnappers left him tied up, he would probably have frozen to death in the forest where he was dumped.

At the forefront of the call for democracy and shaping public opinion was the center-left newspaper *El País*, which was launched on May 4, 1976, with a former political prisoner and a former minister under Franco among its shareholders. Readers in the newspaper's early days who proudly tucked their copy under their arms were known as *sobacos ilustrados* (illustrated armpits). Today, *El País* is the country's largest-selling newspaper, with a circulation of more than 300,000. The minister was Manuel Fraga, who had been responsible, as information and tourism minister, for the 1966 Press Law, which did away with prior censorship. The prisoner was Ramón Tamames, an economics professor and member of the Spanish Communist Party's central committee. The newspaper's chief editorial writer and columnist was Javier Pradera (1934–2011), a Communist during the 1950s whose father and grandfather, both of them part of the conservative establishment, were assassinated by anarchists at the beginning of the Civil War. *El País*, sympathetic to the Socialist Party, challenged the democratic credentials of the first post-Franco government, headed by Carlos Arias Navarro, on its very first day of publication and published the first-ever interview in a Spanish publication with Dolores Ibárruri, the octogenarian president of the Spanish Communist Party, then still in exile in Moscow. On October 18, another newspaper was launched, *Diario 16*, which came out with an editorial demanding the dismantling of the Information Ministry: "The Ministry lives on as flagrant proof that censorship, though muted, still survives." On November 18, Franco's last parliament voted itself out of office by approving political reform and paving the way for a general election in June 1977. *Diario 16* reported the move on its front page with the striking headline "Adiós Dictadura" (Good-bye dictatorship).

What were the main economic problems?

The 15-year period of strong economic growth during which the real GDP increased by close to 7 percent a year, albeit from a low starting point, came to an end after the oil price shock of 1973–1974. The higher prices were particularly damaging for Spain because of its heavy reliance on oil and gas, which supplied over two-thirds of its energy requirements. Industry was energy-intensive, and despite the liberalization ushered in by the 1959 Stabilization Plan (see "What role did the 1959 Stabilization Plan play in creating a modern economy"? in chapter 2) was still among the most protected and least competitive in Western Europe. The economy grew by only one percent in 1975, the year that Franco died.

Inflation rose from 17.4 percent in 1974 to 24.5 percent in 1977, fueled by a wage rise that had run ahead of the increase in consumer prices for several years. The current account, after years of being in surplus, went into deficit as earnings from tourism and remittances from workers abroad stopped offsetting the trade deficit. The number of unemployed more than doubled between 1973 and 1977, to 832,000 (6.3 percent of the labor force), as companies laid off workers to cope with the economic slump. The rise in the jobless rate was also pushed up by the return of emigrants who had lost their jobs. The shipbuilding sector, the world's third largest in 1974, was hard hit by the collapse of the tanker market, and the steel industry, the world's 13th largest, suffered from the world-wide glut in steelmaking capacity. The rise in world oil prices was not passed on to the Spanish consumer as quickly as it was in many other countries, out of fear of stoking inflation even more and intensifying social unrest in the last year of the dictatorship. Consumption of oil continued to grow as if nothing had happened; of the 10 leading Western industrial countries, Spain was the only one in which oil consumption increased.

The public sector was also bloated, with around 1.5 million people on the state payroll, including 250,000 workers employed in more than 60 firms owned or controlled by the loss-making Instituto Nacional de Industria (INI), the state holding company, in sectors such as steel, shipbuilding, and coal.

The first post-Franco government largely ignored the economic problems, as it had enough on its plate with political problems. The second and third governments, led by Adolfo Suárez of the Union of the Democratic Center, did little until the peseta was devalued in February 1976 (by 11 percent) and again in July 1977 (by 20 percent). But these measures did not tackle the roots of the problems, which were structural and required, like the pact between the reformist right and the left that achieved the transition to democracy, a consensus agreement among the political parties, trade unions, and employers. This consensus came in October 1977 with the Moncloa Pacts.

What were the 1977 Moncloa Pacts?

The Moncloa Pacts, named after the prime minister's official residence on the outskirts of Madrid, were an attempt to repeat in the economic field what had been achieved through consensus in the political sphere: essentially to agree on ways to control spiraling inflation and balance-of-payments problems. The mounting economic crisis threatened to blow the march to democracy off course.

The left, which controlled the two main trade unions, agreed to limit wage increases to no more than the expected rate of inflation (previously raises were based on past inflation) in return for various benefits, including better unemployment benefits and pensions; improvements in education, the health service, and housing programs; and a promise to return the assets of the trade unions confiscated after the Civil War.

The first step toward creating a modern tax system was taken when parliament unified the income tax system so that wage earners and non–wage earners were assessed according to the same rules and, for the first time, tax evasion was outlawed. Under Franco, tax avoidance was widespread—total tax revenue in 1975, including contributions to the social security system, represented 18 percent of the GDP, a smaller proportion than in any other OECD country except Turkey. Tax inspectors were recruited and computers employed. As a result of the reforms, the number of taxpayers almost tripled between 1977 and 1979, to 5.3 million.

The Moncloa Pacts' measures, coupled with the devaluation of the peseta in July 1977, lowered inflation to 15 percent over the next three years (still nearly twice the OECD average) and produced the first surplus in the balance of payments since 1973. But the measures were unable to stem the rise in unemployment, and more than one million jobs were lost between 1978 and 1982. The pacts were followed by other agreements between the government and social partners, including the Workers' Statute of 1980, which achieved a degree of social peace. In addition to their economic importance, the pacts were significant in that they showed Spaniards that politicians of different ideologies could come together to solve the country's problems.

What form did the 1978 Constitution take?

The 1978 Constitution, drawn up by a committee of representatives from all the main political parties and approved in a referendum by 88 percent of voters and a turnout of 67 percent, sealed the transition to democracy. It was the sixth constitution since 1812, including the one in 1834 (technically known as a royal statute) and Franco's seven Fundamental Laws, promulgated between 1938 and 1967. They were a kind of constitution, albeit a rather strange one. The average duration of the constitutions between 1812 and 1931 was 17 years. The longest was the constitution of 1876, established after the First Republic and the restoration of the Borbón monarchy under Alfonso XII. It lasted until 1923, when Alfonso XIII turned to General Miguel Primo de Rivera to head the government.

The 1978 Constitution took into account a wide spectrum of political opinion, and as a result each new government since then did not feel the need to mold it to its particular interests. It was drawn up by a committee of seven politicians representing the Union of the Democratic Center (three members), the Socialists (one), the Communists (one), the neo-Francoist Popular Alliance (one), and Catalan and Basque nationalists (one, a Catalan politician). It has hardly been changed since it was approved.

The constitution consolidated the monarchy as reinstated by Franco and the parliamentary system that the Political Reform Law of November 1976 put into effect. This turned Franco's Cortes into a two-chamber parliament, with a 350-seat congress elected by universal suffrage and a 250-member senate chosen by a mixture of election and appointment (41 by King Juan Carlos). As regards basic human and social rights and the rule of law, the fathers of the constitution drew on its

1931 democratic precursor, produced by the Second Republic (1931–1936), though without directly referring to it so as to avoid inflaming the right and killing the carefully nurtured spirit of consensus. The constitution paved the way for a quasi-federal system with 17 autonomous communities, ending the very centralized state that Franco had created and that the military was charged with defending.

The other controversial issue in the writing of the constitution was the role of the powerful Catholic Church, a pillar of the Franco regime. Both the UCD government, with the support of the left-wing opposition parties, and the church's hierarchy, led by the liberal Cardinal Vicente Enrique y Tarancón, the archbishop of Madrid and head of the Episcopal Conference (the bishops' organization), adopted a moderate strategy of consensus. No one wanted to evoke the conflicts that afflicted the Republic. Anticlericalism was one of the factors that inspired Franco's uprising in 1936, which the church blessed as a "crusade." Whereas the 1931 Constitution declared that Spain had no official religion, the 1978 Constitution stated that "there shall be no state religion," and Article 16:3 declared: "the public authorities shall take the religious beliefs of Spanish society into account and shall in consequence maintain appropriate cooperation with the Catholic Church and the other confessions." No other religious group is mentioned by name. The Socialists saw this as introducing "covert confessionality" and voted against it in the committee that drafted the text.

A small minority of conservative bishops, led by Cardinal Marcelo González Martín, who issued a pastoral letter, criticized the final text of the constitution because it took a position of neutrality on Catholic values, instead of embodying them. The constitution did not combat divorce, birth control, and abortion, all of which were more prevalent in society after the end of the Franco regime. The letter foreshadowed conflicts that would surface during the Socialist governments (see the questions on the church in chapters 4 and 6). In 1979, agreements between the Spanish state and the Holy See, taking the status of international treaties, were signed. The government agreed to continue to pay clerical salaries, while the church promised to pay its own way within three years—a condition still not fulfilled in 2013. State funding of the church's extensive network of schools remained in force, as did religious instruction in public schools, given by teachers chosen by bishops. However, the principle of liberty of conscience for students in public schools was recognized, which meant pupils could no longer be obligated to attend religion classes. The church also received tax benefits.

How and why was the system of regional autonomy created?

A constant theme in Spanish history, and one still not resolved, has been the center-periphery tension between Madrid and the more nationalist regions, particularly the Basque Country and Catalonia. The British author Gerald Brenan (1894–1987), who lived most of his life in Spain, observed that a Spaniard's allegiance was "first of all to his native place, or to his family or social group in it, and only secondly to his country and government." The 1978 Constitution sought to defuse antagonism in the politically charged post-Franco years by creating a system of 17 *comunidades autónomas* (autonomous communities), which turned Spain into a quasi-federal state.

A significant part of the pressure for change during the transition to democracy came from the Basque Country (comprising administratively the provinces of Guipuzcoa, Vizcaya, and Alava) and Catalonia. During the Second Republic (1931–1939), both enjoyed a measure of self-rule that was suppressed when General Franco won the Civil War in 1939 and created one of the most rigidly centralized states in Europe. Galicia also had a statute of autonomy, but it could not be implemented because of the conflict.

Adolfo Suárez, the prime minister between 1976 and 1981, started the devolution process in 1977 when he invited Josep Tarradellas, the 78-year-old head of the Catalan government-in-exile, back to Spain to assume the presidency of the reestablished Generalitat, the traditional government of Catalonia dating back to the 13th century, in which he had served during the Civil War. Tarradellas, in return, promised to recognize the monarchy and the unity of Spain.

The 1978 Constitution acknowledged the existence of "nationalities" and "regions," but preferred not to list them for fear of upsetting sensibilities. Varying degrees of power were gradually devolved to the communities and the North African enclaves of Ceuta and Melilla between 1979 and 1983, while maintaining, in the words of the constitution, the "indissoluble unity of the Spanish Nation." The central government retained control of foreign policy, trade, defense, and macroeconomic policy, while the communities were gradually given responsibility for education, housing, health, and justice. This widespread devolution was known as *café para todos* (coffee for everyone) and led to the creation of bloated regional bureaucracies and around 5,000 companies owned by regions or town halls, from TV channels to garbage collectors and foundations, that caused Spain's budget deficit and public debt to balloon. The fiscal model for the regions was flawed from the start: revenue is essentially in the hands of the central government and spending in those of the 17 regional governments.

The Basque Country, where the violent separatist group ETA continued to fight for independence, was not directly represented in the seven-man committee that drafted the 1978 Constitution. All the regions were represented by a Catalan. All of the amendments of the center-right Partido Nacionalista Vasco (PNV, Basque Nationalist Party) to the constitutional text were rejected. Among other things, the PNV wanted recognition of the Basque Country's *foral* (historical) rights. This led to the party's withdrawal from the larger parliamentary body overseeing the constitution and an abstention rate of 46 percent in the Basque Country when the constitution was put to a nationwide referendum in December 1978 compared to a rate of 33 percent for the whole of Spain. The combined

Basque "no" vote and abstentions totaled 57 percent. To this day, the PNV, and radical Basque nationalist parties even more so, declare no allegiance to the constitution. The reasons invoked for the rejection lay in the non-recognition of the right to self-determination and assignation of the role of guarantor of the territorial integrity of Spain to the army.

In July 1979, Adolfo Suárez, the prime minister, reached an agreement with the PNV on a system of self-government for the provinces of Guipuzcoa, Vizcaya, and Alava, which became the autonomous community of the Basque Country. Suarez gave the Basques a greater degree of self-government than they received through the 1936 statute and more than that of any other Spanish region. The Basques received their own tax system (they transfer a prearranged amount to the central government every year) and police force. Suarez hoped this would pacify the region. The Basques approved the deal in a referendum in October 1979. A similar status was agreed for the adjoining region of Navarre. The ETA, however, carried on killing until October 2011, when it declared a "definitive" cease-fire but did not lay down its arms (see "Why was a 'dirty war' waged against the Basque terrorist group ETA?" in chapter 4).

How different are the regions?

The 17 regions vary considerably in size, economic structure, and wealth. Andalusia, with a population of 8.5 million (almost one-fifth of Spain's), is the largest region and, along with Extremadura, which borders Portugal, the poorest. Unemployment rates in these two regions were more than 30 percent in 2013, compared to a national average of over 25 percent. There were lower levels of unemployment in the northern regions, accentuating the country's north-south divide.

The predominant economic activity in Andalusia is tourism, particularly on its Costa del Sol, and in Extremadura it is agriculture. Madrid is the seat of the central government, the headquarters of many Spanish and foreign companies and the nation's capital; Catalonia in the northeast is an economic powerhouse and accounts for one-quarter of exports (its economy is the size of Portugal's); La Rioja in the north is famous for its wines; Galicia in the northwest is legendary for its rain; and the Canary Islands are closer to Africa than to the rest of Europe.

Regional stereotypes abound: the people of Madrid are viewed as flashy, Andalusians as revelers, the Catalans as stingy, and Galicians are so enigmatic that if met on a staircase "you can't tell if they are going up or down," according to a popular saying. The Basque Country, Catalonia, and Galicia have their own languages.

Spaniards in the wealthier northern regions tend to look down on their compatriots in the south for being lazy and too dependent on transfers of funds from Madrid under the so-called solidarity system to level out regional income disparities. This is particularly the case of Catalans, who resent the amount of transfers they must pay to the central government for distribution to the poorer regions. Following a snap election in the region in November 2012, parties in favor of a referendum on independence (declared illegal by the central government) won a majority of the seats in the regional parliament and began to push for the creation of a Catalan state.

Nationalism was on the rise, and not just in Catalonia. The 12 nationalist parties (i.e., those that only ran candidates in their regions) captured 12.3 percent of the vote in the November 2011 general election and 43 of the 350 seats, up from 8.6 percent and 27, respectively, by the 10 nationalist parties in the 2008 election. If one adds the Partido Socialista de Catalonia (Catalan Socialist Party, PSC), affiliated to the Socialist party, and the Unión del Pueblo Navarro (Navarrese People's Union, UPN), allied to the PP, both of which ran candidates only in their regions, these parties gained 16.1 percent of the vote and 59 seats in 2011 (15.6 percent and 54 in 2008).

Why did the ETA continue its violent campaign for an independent Basque state?

The October 1979 autonomy statute for the Basque Country, approved in a referendum, and the formation of a nationalist government in 1980 in the region did not stop the ETA from continuing to kill in the name of an independent Basque state. The group killed 92 people in 1980, its bloodiest year, compared to 70 between 1968 and 1977. The Partido Nacionalista Vasco (PNV, Basque Nationalist Party) and Herri Batasuna, the ETA's political wing, won between them a majority of the parliamentary seats in the 1980 election. As far as the ETA's gunmen were concerned, democracy was nothing but a cosmetic change in the authoritarian nature of the Spanish state. The group still regarded the state as an occupying force. Its victims were not just representatives of the state, but also some businessmen and politicians. The ETA's cause was aided by the extreme brutality of the Civil Guard during the dictatorship, which, according to Amnesty International, changed very little in the first years of democracy. Many Basques with no connections to terrorism who were arrested after the death of Franco emerged from prison bearing the marks of torture. Some ETA suspects, such as José Arregui in 1981, died in custody. His death triggered a strike in the Basque Country.

The ETA's legitimacy was also boosted by the "dirty war" that elements in the Socialist government of Felipe González waged against it between 1983 and 1987. The war erupted when a group called GAL (Grupos Antiterroristas de Liberación, Anti-Terrorist Liberation Groups) killed 27 people, including 10 whose connections to the ETA were unclear or did not exist (see "Why was a 'dirty war' waged against the Basque terrorist group ETA?" in chapter 4).

Why was there an attempted coup in 1981?

The legalization of the Communist Party, the creation of a quasi-federal system for the regions, the mounting violence of the Basque separatist group ETA that killed more than 240 people between 1977 and 1981, and a growing economic crisis was too much for recalcitrant Francoists to swallow. On February 23, 1981, a group of Civil Guards, led by an officer with a bushy moustache and wearing the tricorne (three-cornered hat), seized the parliament during the televised process of Leopoldo Calvo Sotelo's election to replace Adolfo Suárez as prime minister. Suárez had resigned as a result of divisions within the Union of the Democratic Center, a disparate coalition.

During the coup Lt. Col. Antonio Tejero burst into the parliament firing shots into the air, while in Valencia the captain-general of the Valencia military region, Jaime Milans del Bosch, declared a state of emergency and sent tanks into the city. General Manuel Gutiérrez Mellado, the deputy prime minister for defense, confronted Tejero, a known plotter against democracy, but was manhandled back into his seat by him. All the members of parliament dived under their desks for cover except Suárez, Gutiérrez Mellado, and the Communist leader Santiago Carrillo, key protagonists of the transition to democracy. Civil Guardsmen escorted Carrillo to a back room and threatened him with execution. Javier Cercas analyzes this defining moment in his brilliant book *The Anatomy of a Moment*. Images of the coup flashed on televisions around the country, and within hours those leading members of the opposition not stuck in parliament went into hiding. Thousands of Spaniards, fearing the worst, headed in their cars for France and Portugal.

Tejero, involved in Operation Galaxia, the code name given to an earlier coup plan in 1978, which was revealed to the authorities and for which he served only seven months' detention, believed he had the support of King Juan Carlos, but this was not the case. The plotters included General Alfonso Armada, a former secretary-general of the royal household. The coup collapsed the next day after the king, wearing the full regalia of commander-in-chief of the armed forces, denounced it in a nationwide broadcast on television.

"The crown...cannot tolerate in any form actions or attitudes of persons who try to interrupt the democratic process of the Constitution." Had he not done otherwise, it would have been the end of the monarchy and even that of the new democracy. Millions of people around Spain celebrated the failed coup. The bullet holes in the parliament's ceiling were kept as a chilling reminder of how perilously close Spain had come to turning back the clock.

4

THE SOCIALIST ERA, 1982–1996

Why did the Socialists win a landslide victory in the 1982 election?

The Unión del Centro Democrático (UCD, the Union of the Democratic Center), a disparate coalition held together by an ambition for power rather than a common ideology, imploded in the run-up to the October 1982 election. This occurred as a result of divisions and defections by some of its leaders to other parties on the left and right, mostly the latter. The UCD served its purpose as a vehicle for overseeing the transition and preventing polarization. Nevertheless, once democracy was secured it ceased to have a useful role and its constituent parts splintered. Its disintegration can also be interpreted as a sign of the consolidation and maturity of the political system as it would not have happened if both the political elites and citizens still feared the polarization that justified its creation.

The Partido Socialista Obrero Español (PSOE, the Spanish Socialist Workers' Party) had by then emerged under the charismatic leadership of Felipe González. It had a moderate social democrat platform that appealed to the left-of-center sociological majority of the electorate, particularly those born after the 1936–1939 Civil War. Furthermore, it did not antagonize the armed forces, smarting from the failed coup in February 1981, except the most reactionary officers. The Socialists caught the mood of the country with their slogan *por el cambio* (time for change) and won 48.3 percent of the vote in the election and 202 of the 350 seats in parliament. This is still the largest majority ever enjoyed by any party, including during the Second Republic. The voter turnout of the 1982 election, 80 percent, has also not been exceeded since. The second-largest victory went to the right-wing Alianza Popular (AP, Popular Alliance) in an alliance with the Partido Demócrata Popular (PDP, Democratic Popular Party) headed by Manuel Fraga, with 26.5 percent of the votes and 107 seats, followed by the center-right Catalan nationalist Convergència i Unió (CiU, Convergence and Union) with 3.7 percent and 12 seats, the UCD (6.8 percent and 11 seats), the Partido Nacionalista Vasco (PNV, Basque Nationalist Party) with 1.9 percent and eight seats, and, finally, the Communists received 4 percent and four seats. The adoption of the province as the electoral district meant that the proportional effects of the Hondt system were distorted to favor regional concentration of votes. As a result, the CiU won more seats than the UCD, although it obtained a smaller share of votes.

The election marked a turning point. King Juan Carlos reportedly said democracy would not be secured until the Socialists, traditionally a republican party, were in power. They remained in power under González until 1996. The election ushered in an essentially two-party political system, between the Socialists and the AP, later the Partido Popular (PP, Popular Party; see "How did the right reinvent itself and return to power in 1996 under the Popular Party?" in chapter 5), which remains to this day.

Who is Felipe González?

Felipe González, prime minister between 1982 and 1996, was born in Seville in 1942 during the repressive decade that followed General Franco's victory in the 1936–1939 Civil War. The son of a dairy farmer, González attended a school run by the Claretian missionaries and took a law degree. While at university, he was involved with Catholic political groups under the tutelage of Manuel Giménez Fernández, a Christian Democrat professor who had been a CEDA minister in 1934 during the Second Republic. In 1965, the German Catholic Church gave González a scholarship to study economics at the Catholic University of Louvain in Belgium where he saw at first hand the hard conditions of Spanish emigrants.

He began his career as a labor relations lawyer in Seville and was active in reviving the clandestine Partido Socialista Obrero Español (PSOE, the Spanish Socialist Workers' Party) under the nom de guerre of Isidoro. He gained prominence at the PSOE's congress in Toulouse, France, in August 1972 along with other young militants from Spain, such as Alfonso Guerra, who began to challenge the exiled and elderly leadership of Rodolfo Llopis (1895–1983) for being out of touch with the changes that had taken place in Spain. Two years later, in October, González wrested control of the party from Llopis at the congress in Suresnes near Paris and was elected secretary-general.

González took a pragmatic approach to the transition from its early stages, realizing that an abrupt break with the dictatorship, known as *ruptura democrática* (democratic break), was impossible and change would come only from negotiations with the government. Willy Brandt, the social democrat chancellor of West Germany, was an influential political mentor for González. Brandt had covered the Civil War as a journalist. The party's victory in the April 1979 municipal elections, the first democratic ones at the local level since the Second Republic, convinced González that if the PSOE shed its traditional ideological baggage as a Marxist party and occupied the social democrat ground it could win the general election. The Marxist tag gave the Socialists' enemies on the right plenty of ammunition to attack it and scare away potential voters.

In a bold move, González resigned as secretary-general at the PSOE's congress in May 1979 after the committee responsible for the ideological definition reaffirmed it as Marxist. He spent the summer touring Spain and explaining his position to rank-and-file party members and returned as secretary-general at the extraordinary congress in September when his opponents were massively outvoted. He was greatly helped in this maneuver by Guerra, a close associate from their university days in Seville. Guerra exercised an iron control over the party apparatus and became deputy prime minister after the Socialists won the 1982 election. The average age of ministers in the first Socialist government was just over 40, and many of them had received part of their education abroad. González won four elections, but bowed out of day-to-day politics after losing in 1996.

How did the Socialists come to grips with the dire economic situation?

The Socialists inherited an economy in the last part of 1982 that had been barely growing for three years and had high rates of unemployment (15.6 percent) and inflation. The economy was heavily dependent on imported oil, much of industry and many banks were uncompetitive, agriculture was inefficient, and the labor laws, designed in the Franco regime to protect employment in return for political obedience, were rigid and hindered job creation. The Socialists had promised during their electoral campaign to create 800,000 new jobs during their first four-year term of office, but quickly realized that this was unrealistic. Roughly the same number of jobs were lost by the time the next election was held in June 1986.

The Socialists had learned a lesson from the ruinous French experience. Felipe González, the prime minister, did not follow the example of François Mitterrand, the French president (1981–1995) who nationalized companies and banks, raised the minimum wage, shortened the working week, created 250,000 new government jobs, and imposed a "solidarity tax" on the rich. These policies aggravated rather than resolved France's macroeconomic imbalances, and Mitterrand shifted to more orthodox policies that restored health to the economy. There was only one nationalization in the Spanish Socialists' program and that was Red Eléctrica de España, the power grid. Their very first major action, however, was the expropriation in February 1983 of Rumasa, the largest private holding company embracing banking, construction, drinks, hotels, insurance, and urban and agricultural property, on the grounds that it was teetering on the edge of bankruptcy and the government needed to protect the banking system and around 60,000 jobs.

The industrial crisis of the late 1970s had hit the Spanish financial sector hard; of the 110 banks in the country between 1977 and 1985, 58 of them suffered problems of one type or another. Rumasa's companies were later privatized, as were, in the second half of the 1980s, various companies of the Instituto Nacional de Industria (INI, the National Institute of Industry), most notably Seat, the loss-making car manufacturer, which was sold to Germany's Volkswagen, and Ensasa (trucks), was sold to Iveco, a division of Italy's Fiat, in order to guarantee their survival. When the Socialists took office, INI, founded in 1941 as the driving force behind the Franco regime's policy of economic self-sufficiency, had 217,000 employees (7 percent of the industrial labor force) and accounted for all of the country's output of aircraft and aluminum, 80 percent of its ships, 50 percent of its coal, 40 percent of its fertilizers, and a third of its steel and electricity. The large and inefficient heavy industries, mainly in the north of Spain, such as shipbuilding and steel, were massively slimmed down. The big profitable state companies regarded as strategic, such as Telefónica (telecommunications), Repsol (oil and gas), and Endesa (electricity), were partially privatized between 1988 and 1995 through initial public offerings in order to prepare them for greater competition.

The peseta was devalued by 8 percent, monetary policy tightened, and the Socialists' sister trade union, the Unión General de Trabajadores (UGT, General Union of Workers), and the Communist-dominated Comisiones Obreras (CC OO,

Workers' Commissions) exercised wage restraint. Economic policy was in the hands of Miguel Boyer, an economist who had worked in the Bank of Spain (the central bank). The ailing and state-owned steel and shipbuilding industries were streamlined with the help of government aid, and the state oil, tobacco, and cereal monopolies began to be dismantled.

In the labor market sphere, the government introduced a fixed-term contract while keeping virtually untouched the Franco regime's paternalist employment protection legislation for permanent workers. This new contract, which had to last for at least six months and could be renewed for up to three years, was seized upon by employers as a way to get around the rigid labor laws. Employers reckoned it cost a company almost twice as much to fire a worker on a permanent contract in Spain as the European norm. The share of the workforce on these precarious temporary contracts shot up from less than 10 percent before 1984 to 33 percent in 2007 at the peak of the economic boom and created a dual labor market split between insiders (those in a privileged situation on permanent contracts) and outsiders (those on fixed-term contracts). The still-dysfunctional labor market is one factor behind Spain's persistently high unemployment.

A turnaround came in 1985 when inflation dipped below 10 percent for the first time in a decade and an export boom and large inflows of foreign direct investment helped the current account swing into surplus. The foundations were laid for another sustained period of high economic growth, similar to that in the 1960s. The economy grew by an annual average of 4.5 percent in real terms between 1986 and 1990, well above the 3.3 percent for the then 15 countries of the European Economic Community, and the unemployment rate fell from 20 percent to 16 percent during this period. Carlos Solchaga, the economy and finance minister, boasted in 1988 that Spain was the country where one could become rich the most quickly.

Relations between the government and trade unions deteriorated, however, particularly with the UGT. Nicolás Redondo, the UGT secretary-general who had passed up the opportunity to be the Socialists' leader at the Suresnes (France) congress in 1974, resigned his seat in parliament in October 1987 in protest against the restrictive 1988 budget. The unions, particularly angered by the reform of the state pension system and new labor contracts for young adults with less redundancy pay, wanted a *giro social* (a U-turn to the left) involving greater redistribution of the wealth being created and a more fully developed welfare state. They staged a general strike in December 1988. Accused by Redondo of favoring the rich, González replied: "My problem is not that there are rich people, it is that there are poor people."

Trade union membership dropped during the 1980s, even though there was freedom to join them, from 21 percent of salaried workers to 13 percent, well below the average of 28 percent for OECD countries. This happened as a result of the changes to the economy, particularly the growing importance of the services sector, where unions tend to be weak.

Why and how were the armed forces reformed?

The coup on February 23, 1981 (known as 23-F), which came close to reversing Spain's march to democracy, underscored the urgency of military reform. While other institutions, most notably the parliament, had become democratic and a liberal constitution was in place as of 1978, the mentality of the military top brass had hardly changed. Alberto Oliart, the defense minister after the coup in the last government of the Union of the Democratic Center, summed up the mind-set in the following way: "The military only has two elementary ideas about politics: one, communism is enemy number one; two, Spain is different to other countries and democracy is impossible."

As the main pillar of the regime, the armed forces were top-heavy with generals whose only loyalty was to Francoism. When a defense ministry was created in June 1977 out of the army, navy, and air force ministries and headed by a civilian as of 1979, the newspaper *El Alcázar*, the mouthpiece of the ultra-right-wing and named after a famous siege during the Civil War, declared that the ministry "does not represent the armed forces." Of the 114 ministers who had served in Franco's governments between 1939 and 1975, 40 of them were military men. In 1980, five years after the dictator's death, the army still had a disproportionate number of generals, at 565. Most of them were over the age of 73, which meant they were in their 30s when they fought on Franco's side during the 1936–1939 Civil War. Every single member of the Consejo Superior del Ejército de Tierra (Superior Council of the Army) at the time of Franco's death had fought in the war. The military also had its own courts, which were used to try a wide range of political crimes.

Lower down the ranks, some younger officers, commissioned after 1960 and less indoctrinated, belonged to the clandestine Unión Democrática Militar (UMD, Democratic Military Union), formed during the last years of the dictatorship. Nine of its members were arrested in July 1975 and given prison sentences of up to eight years. Ironically, one of them had been born inside the Alcázar fortress in Toledo during its protracted siege in 1936 by Republican forces in the Civil War. After Franco's victory, the military turned a room in the fortress (now the Army Museum) into a shrine, with a telephone and portraits of Col. José Moscardó, the military governor of Toledo, and his young son, Luis, who was taken prisoner elsewhere in Spain by Republican soldiers. Moscardó, who held out for 70 days in the Alcázar until Franco's forces arrived, was called on the telephone and told his son would be shot unless he surrendered the fortress. He asked to speak to his son and told him to "commend your soul to God and die like a patriot, shouting 'Long live Christ the King' and 'Long live Spain.'"

Alfonso Guerra, the deputy prime minister in the Socialist government that took office in December 1982, explained the government's position toward the military as one "founded on loyalty but always on the firm basis of respect for government authority." The Socialists stamped their authority by appointing Narcís Serra, a Catalan politician and former mayor of Barcelona, as defense minister. Serra, who managed as a young man to avoid the compulsory military service, spent nine years in the post modernizing the armed forces and moving its primary role away from internal security and toward national defense. There was no purge of die-hard Francoist military or police officers, in keeping with the spirit of the transition to democracy that dictated not seeking revenge. (When González went to Seville for the first time as prime minister, he was received in the airport by the same policeman who had arrested him in 1974, after he was elected secretary-general of the Socialists at the party's congress in France.)

In 1984, the new defense law gave the prime minister greater authority over the armed forces, aided by the creation of a National Defense Board and a reformed Joint Chiefs of Staff, which became a consultative and not a command body. A new military code came into force in 1985 limiting its jurisdiction to military crimes. These reforms ended more than 100 years of the military's autonomy from the government and subordinated the armed forces to civilian power. The size of the armed forces was reduced from more than 300,000 at the time of Franco's death (217,000 conscripts) to 217,000 (158,000 conscripts) in 1991, by which time the term of compulsory military service had been cut from one year to nine months. It was abolished in 2001. The reduced size lowered the proportion of the military budget spent on personnel (two-thirds in the mid-1970s, much higher than in other Western European countries) and freed up money for better equipment and matériel.

Why did the Socialists oppose NATO membership and then make a U-turn?

The Socialists froze participation in NATO, approved by the previous government of the Union of the Democratic Center in 1981, which had pushed it through parliament with little consultation, and stuck to their campaign pledge to hold a referendum on the issue. The move irritated other NATO members, particularly the United States, which feared Spain's withdrawal could set a precedent for other countries, such as Greece, whose membership was regarded as shaky.

Unlike on the issue of European Union membership, there was no broad consensus in Spain over joining NATO. It was a particularly contentious issue for the left, which saw it as aggravating the Cold War environment. Washington's support for the Franco regime, embodied in the 1953 bases agreement (see "Why was the 1953 military bases agreement with the United States important?" in chapter 2), fostered feelings of betrayal and a strong streak of anti-American sentiment toward US foreign policy among Spanish democrats. This was exemplified almost 30 years later when the Spanish parliament was seized during the February 1981 coup. Instead of rallying to the support of the beleaguered democratic government, the US secretary of state, Alexander Haig, a former general, called it "a Spanish internal affair." This remark confirmed the belief of the Spanish left that Washington placed little importance on the fate of Spanish democracy and still hankered after the cozy relationship it had enjoyed during the Franco regime. The left was also antagonized by the heavy-handed US intervention in Central America during the early 1980s, following the Sandinista overthrow of the Washington-backed dictatorship of Anastasio Somoza in Nicaragua and Washington's subsequent covert support for the Contras fighting the rebels.

González realized NATO membership was an inherent part of the country's integration into Western Europe and would help to end Spain's isolation. It would also aid the modernization and depoliticization of the armed forces. After Spain joined the EU in January 1986, he decided to hold the referendum in March and, in a remarkably bold policy U-turn, campaigned for a "yes" vote. The Socialists' slogan was *OTAN en el interés de España* ("NATO in the interest of Spain") and they won the day (53 percent in favor and 40.3 percent against), but the abstention rate was high at 40 percent. Despite its long support for NATO membership, the conservative Alianza Popular (AP, Popular Alliance), headed by Manuel Fraga, urged voters to abstain. Fraga's opportunistic gamble was that González would lose the referendum and have to call fresh elections, which the AP would win.

The Socialists attached three conditions to their "yes vote": Spain would not join NATO's military command structure; the ban on nuclear weapons in Spain would remain; and, most important, there would be a gradual reduction of the US military presence in Spain. For the Socialists, overcoming the Francoist origin of the 1953 military bases agreement with the US could only be achieved by reducing the US presence in Spain—rather than just by joining NATO. Francisco Fernández Ordóñez, the foreign minister, put the position clearly when he told US Secretary of State George Shultz: "What we want is a balanced relationship between equals, not subordination."

This was accomplished by a new agreement regarding military bases in 1988, which reduced the US presence by around 40 percent (4,500 military personnel and 500 civilians) and removed the 72 F-16 fighter bombers from Torrejón on the outskirts of Madrid. Despite the limitations on Spain's NATO membership, a formula was developed that enabled the country to make its contribution to Western security through a set of coordination agreements. Unlike France, which also stayed out of the military command structure, Spain participated in the Defense Planning Committee, the Military Committee, and the Nuclear Plan Group (NPG), and took part in the Alliance's defense planning process. During the 1990 Gulf War, the Socialists gave US forces en route to the area unlimited use of their military facilities in Spain and sent Spanish naval units to the region under the framework of the Western European Union, which Spain joined that year in order to participate in the embargo imposed by the UN Security Council. The conservative Popular Party, which ousted the Socialists in 1996, integrated Spain into NATO's military command structure in

1999, at which time Javier Solana, the former Socialist foreign minister, had been NATO secretary-general for four years. Interestingly, Solana wrote a pamphlet against NATO when he was a young man.

What was the impact of European Economic Community membership?

The Franco regime had applied to join the then European Economic Community (EEC) in 1962, but there was no way this would happen until Spain became a democracy. The request received a cool reception from the European Commission, which only acknowledged receipt of the letter. The regime tried again in 1964 when the commission was authorized to examine economic issues with Spain. This led to a preferential trade pact in 1970.

Once the dictatorship ended in 1975 and the country was set on a democratic course, the way was open for full membership. All political parties, except those on the extreme right, were in favor of joining the EEC (known as the European Union since 1993), as it signified Spain finally coming out of the cold and being fully embraced by the wider democratic European community. Spain was admitted to the Council of Europe in November 1977, two years after Franco's death, a kind of anteroom to the EEC. Accession negotiations began in February 1979 and were complicated and protracted. Spain's level of economic development was significantly lower than that of the 10 other member nations, except for Greece, and its industrial sector was in need of profound structural reform. There were also difficulties concerning Spain's fishing fleets. It was in the area of agriculture, however, that the potential consequences of Spanish membership created the greatest concern, particularly in France, which viewed Spain as a threat to the livelihood of its farmers. Spain's agriculture sector as a whole was inefficient (it employed around 20 percent of the workforce but produced only 6 percent of the GDP), but had competitive exporters of fruit and vegetables.

The accession agreement, which came into force in January 1986, established a seven-year transition period covering areas such as the removal of customs duties and industrial tariffs on EEC goods and the removal of Spanish import levies and most quotas. Longer-term arrangements were made for the inclusion of Spain's agricultural sector in the Common Agricultural Policy (CAP), and membership of the European Monetary System (EMS) was delayed until the Spanish government felt the economy was fully prepared.

The impact of membership was almost immediately evident. In 1986, the share of total exports going to the EEC rose from 53 to 60 percent in 1985, while the EEC's slice of Spain's import market increased from 36 to 48 percent. West Germany took over from the United States as Spain's largest supplier. The economy became much more open: exports and imports of goods represented 61 percent of the GDP in 1995, up from 27 percent in 1975 and 36 percent in 1985. Foreign direct investment poured in as companies sought to position themselves in a consumer market of some 40 million. Foreign ownership of shares issued by nonfinancial companies increased from 14 percent to 40 percent of the total between 1983 and 1992, and from 5 percent to 22 percent of financial companies.

In order to ease the wrenching economic adjustments that Spain had to make to meet its EEC obligations and the increased competition, Felipe González, the prime minister, became the champion of the poorer EEC members—Portugal, Ireland, and Greece—in addition to Spain. At the December 1992 summit in Edinburgh, González won the EEC's agreement to establish a cohesion fund for countries, like Spain, whose per capita income was less than 90 percent of the EEC average, and an increase in structural funds for poor regions in order to reduce the income disparities between them. Spain benefited considerably from the various types of EEC funds, much of which was used to transform the country's transport infrastructure with the building of motorways, airports, and a high-speed railway network. The 475-kilometer high-speed train track from Madrid to Seville, inaugurated in 1992 to coincide with the World's Fair in the capital of Andalusia, the fiefdom of the Socialist party, cut the travel time between the cities by half, to under three hours.

What was the Socialists' foreign policy?

The main priority of Spain's foreign policy was to integrate into the European Economic Community (EEC) and achieve a more balanced relationship with the United States. Franco's foreign policy was essentially pro-American and pro-Arab; EEC membership was impossible because of his dictatorship.

Britain's support for Spain's EEC membership, once democracy was established, was helped by the Socialists' decision in 1985 to fully open the border with Gibraltar at the southern tip of Spain. Franco had closed the border in 1969 with the then British colony (an overseas UK territory since 2002), over which Spain had long claimed sovereignty. Gibraltar was ceded to Britain in 1713 under the Treaty of Utrecht. The Socialists established diplomatic relations with Israel in 1986, but balanced this relationship by allowing the Palestine Liberation Organization to set up a delegation in Madrid. This completed Spain's return to normal diplomatic relations with all countries. (Relations with the Soviet Union and Mexico, both of which supported the Republic during the Civil War, had been established in 1977 by the centrist government of Adolfo Suárez.)

Once Spain was inside the EEC, the Socialists used their membership to further Spain's role as a natural bridge between Europe and Latin America and foster policies that eased the region's foreign debt repayments and promoted economic growth. (Franco saw Spain's relations with Latin America in terms of a spiritual community of Hispanic nations, a concept known as *Hispanidad*.) Felipe González was actively engaged in the democratization processes in Argentina, Chile, Uruguay, and Central America, where he was able to put to good use his own expertise.

The Socialists opposed the US-backed Contra war against the left-wing Sandinista government of Nicaragua during the 1980s. The Sandinistas had toppled the brutal dictatorship of Anastasio Somoza in 1978. Spanish troops, police, and observers participated in the United Nations' peacekeeping and agreement-verification missions in El Salvador, Nicaragua, and Honduras.

Spain's higher international profile was also exemplified by the fact that in just over a decade it went from receiving official development assistance (ODA) to donating it. In 1992, Spain's ODA represented 0.26 percent of GDP, below the figure of 0.35 percent recommended by the Organization for Economic Co-operation and Development (OECD) for developed countries but well above the minuscule 0.05 percent recorded in 1983.

In 1992, Spain was instrumental in launching the Ibero-American Community of Nations, an intergovernmental organization comparable to the British Commonwealth. It has held annual summits ever since; in 1993 the country became a nonpermanent member of the UN Security Council.

How did the Socialists create a welfare state?

The Spanish welfare state was one of the last to arrive on the European scene. While most European governments were busy between 1960 and 1975 constructing pensions, unemployment benefits, health and housing schemes, and so on, the Franco regime's social expenditure was minimal but still significant. But once democracy was consolidated, particularly after the Socialists came to power in 1982, Spain began racing to catch up. Public spending soared from 24 percent of the GDP in 1975, the year that Franco died, to 40 percent in 1980 and 45 percent in 1994—while in France it increased from

53 percent to 54 percent in the same period, and in Germany from 48 percent to 51 percent.

Government spending went to pay for the surge in public-sector employment (from 1.5 million jobs in 1982 to 2.2 million in 1992) and for social expenses, particularly pensions, where expenditure rose from 1.3 billion pesetas in 1982 to 6.5 billion in 1995 and accounted for one-quarter of total public spending. The 1986 health law established the universalization of health care. By 1994, 80 percent of the population was covered by a network of primary care. The 1990 Law on the General Organization of the Education System (LOGSE) made education compulsory and free in state schools and raised the legal school-leaving age from 14 to 16. This brought Spain into line with most of Europe. The proportion of children between the ages of three and five in preschool rose from 47 percent in 1975 to 84 percent in 1992, and the number of university students increased from 800,000 in 1985 to around 1.5 million in 1995. Unemployment benefits were increased, partly to cope with the surge in unemployment to 24 percent of the workforce in 1994, and subsidies were given for rural underemployment, fostering a large degree of corruption and cronyism in villages.

Spain sought to pay for the surge in expenditure by raising taxes and making the tax-collection system more efficient and by borrowing. Nevertheless, spending outpaced fiscal revenues to such an extent that the general government budget deficit reached 7 percent of the GDP in 1993. The number of people paying income tax increased from 303,000 in 1970 to more than 11 million in 1992, and value-added tax (VAT) was introduced in 1986 as a result of joining the European Union. The state pensions system was reformed because of the rapidly aging population, which strained the government's finances. For every beneficiary of the pension program there were only 2.3 social security contributors, compared with an average of five in the rest of Western Europe. The number of years' contribution required to qualify for the basic state pension was increased from 10 to 15 years and the period for calculating the pension lengthened. The sharp rise in the number of retired people (to around five million in the 1980s) relative to the size of the working population was mainly due to the fall in the fertility rate. Spanish women averaged almost three children in 1960 and only 1.2 in 1992, well below the replacement level of 2.1 and resulting in a relatively stagnant population until the influx of immigrants in the mid-1990s.

This fall in fecundity was the steepest in Europe. The Franco regime, aided by the Catholic Church, promoted large families, abortion was illegal, and contraception was not available. The regime awarded natality prizes every year to couples with the most children. (Franco himself had only one child.) The extended family–based network was and remains, though to a lesser extent than in the past, a cushion, particularly during times of economic crisis. Around two-thirds of unmarried Spaniards aged 25 to 30 live at home, a high figure by European standards, and the number is rising because of very high unemployment and the lack of affordable housing. The network looks after unemployed members, enabling the great majority of pensioners to live with their children and care for grandchildren. As a result, many women are able to work without having to pay for childcare.

How close were the Socialists to meeting the conditions for membership in the European Economic and Monetary Union?

The Spanish economy made great strides after joining the European Economic Community in 1986 (known as the European Union as of 1993), but had a long way to go if the country was to be among the first to join the Economic and Monetary Union (EMU) in 1999 and adopt the euro. The convergence criteria required to enter EMU, which stemmed from the 1992 Maastricht Treaty, were: a budget deficit of no more than 3 percent of the GDP; a maximum public debt level of 60 percent of the GDP; long-term interest rates no higher than 2 percentage points above the average of the three countries with the lowest rates; and inflation no more than 1.5 percentage points higher than the average of the three best-performing countries. As regards the peseta, applicant countries needed to be in the exchange-rate mechanism of the European Monetary System (EMS) for two consecutive years and not have devalued their currency during this period. The Spanish peseta entered the EMS in 1989 with a wide exchange-rate band (6 percent).

The government responded to the EMU challenge with a new program. It doubled the amount of time required to qualify for unemployment benefits from six months to one year; reduced the duration and level of benefits; eliminated telephone, transport, and oil-distribution monopolies; established an anti-trust authority; froze subsidies to state companies; and gave the Bank of Spain, the central bank, independence to set monetary policy.

However, the high growth in public spending, partly motivated by the infrastructure needed for the 1992 Olympic Games in Barcelona and the World's Fair in Seville, created macroeconomic imbalances and an overheated economy. The peseta was devalued by 5 percent in September 1992, the first time in 10 years, in a bid to restore the country's ailing competitiveness. That year Spain was ranked 18th out of 23 countries on the world competitiveness scoreboard, an annual comparative study drawn up by the World Economic Forum. This was the first of three devaluations over almost three years, and it caused the peseta to decline by 35 percent against the German DM and fueled inflation. The economy went into recession in 1993 and shrank 1.2 percent, the steepest fall since the 1959 stabilization program (see "What role did the 1959 Stabilization Plan play in creating a modern economy?" in chapter 2) but very mild compared to the one as of 2009 (see various questions in chapter 6). The budget deficit was 7 percent of the GDP, the level of public debt surpassed 60 percent of the GDP, and interest rates and inflation rose above the EMU requirements. The unemployment rate reached 24 percent in

1994, an unprecedented level for Spain. Real economic growth between 1991 and 1995, the Socialists' last full year in office, dropped to an annual average of 1.3 percent from 4.5 percent in 1986–1990 and for the first time was lower than that of the 15 European Union countries. The economic woes contributed to the Socialists' defeat in the 1996 election. The Partido Popular (PP, Popular Party) was left to pick up the pieces and make an extraordinary final sprint toward EMU (see the "How did the Popular Party meet the conditions to adopt the euro as Spain's currency?" in chapter 5).

What were the Socialists' relations with the Catholic Church?

Both the Socialists and the church had moved on considerably since the left's anticlericalism during the Second Republic (1931–1936) and the entrenched position of the reactionary Catholic hierarchy during the Franco dictatorship (1939–1975). Spanish society and its values had also changed. In 1976 almost two-thirds of those questioned in a Gallup poll described themselves as very or quite practicing believers; 10 years later, only two-fifths still did. The Socialists accepted that Catholicism was a sociological reality (many of its voters were observant Catholics), while the church realized that civil-ecclesiastical relations could not be as cozy in a democracy as they had been during the dictatorship.

Inevitably, however, these relations became more conflictive. The Socialists felt the 1978 Constitution was too ambiguous on the church's position and stopped short of making Spain a truly secular state. Church and state in Spain are not as separate as in France. The Socialists took a tougher line on what they regarded as unjustified concessions toward the church by the centrist government that preceded them. Tensions emerged between the government and the church hierarchy over the legalization of abortion, albeit in strict conditions; the institution of tighter control of church schools receiving state subsidies (known as *centros concertados*); negotiation over clerical salaries paid by the state; and relegation of religion courses in state schools and in the *concertados* to an inferior academic status—as well as the revocation of students' compulsory attendance at religious services.

Pope John Paul II (1978–2005) viewed Spain as a bastion of Catholicism to be defended from growing permissiveness and secularism. He held Opus Dei, a mainly lay, ultraconservative Catholic organization founded by the Spanish priest Josemaría Escrivá de Balaguer (see "What is Opus Dei?" in chapter 2), in high regard. In 1982 the pope granted Opus Dei the status of "personal prelature." The jurisdiction of the prelate is linked not to a territory but over persons wherever they happen to be. It also means the organization is under direct supervision by the Holy See, rather than by local bishops. This unique recognition, the only one in the church for a lay organization, enabled the Opus to operate juridically much as religious orders do, without regard for geographical boundaries. The pope's spokesperson was a Spaniard, Joaquín Navarro Valls, a prominent Opus Dei member. The Vatican beatified Escrivá, the founder of the Opus Dei. This was the final step before sainthood (he was canonized in 2002). Many priests assassinated during the Civil War were also beatified, a move viewed by the Socialists as politically provocative.

Under John Paul the church hierarchy in Spain became more militant and vociferous and less accommodating than during the period of the transition to democracy. The liberal Cardinal Vicente Enrique y Tarancón, the archbishop of Madrid, was succeeded by Ángel Suquía Goicoechea, who was more in step with the Vatican's more conservative orientation. The church mobilized mass demonstrations against laws it opposed, while the right-wing Alianza Popular (AP, Popular Alliance) mounted an offensive in parliament and whipped up hysteria by accusing the Socialists of anticlericalism, particularly over changes in education. The Socialists did not rise to the bait or directly confront the church, but they were not prepared to give it a blank check. Their strategy consisted of interpreting obligations set out in the Constitution and treaties as narrowly as possible and pushing forward with legislation to make Spain more secular. Nevertheless, it was not until the early 1990s that Protestant, Jewish, and Muslim organizations received some of the rights accorded to the Catholic Church. They did not obtain, for example, the same exemption from Value-Added Tax (VAT), nor did they receive the same recognition of their religious holidays. A *modus vivendi* was established over the "religious question" that lasted until the Socialists returned to power in 2004. Then further reforms were made that antagonized the church (see "How did the Catholic Church react to the reforms?" in chapter 6).

What was La Movida Madrileña?

The post-Franco atmosphere of freedom, if not hedonism, was encapsulated by the Movida Madrileña (Madrid scene), a countercultural movement that was born in Madrid during the 1980s and that spread around the country. It was as much about having a good time, particularly *salir de copas*—going out to drink until the early hours—as innovations in pop music, films, and the arts in general. The emblematic and best-known figure is Pedro Almodóvar, the most internationally acclaimed Spanish film director since Luis Buñuel, with his provocative style, outlandish sense of humor, bad taste, and kitsch. The *movida*, at least in cinema terms, dates from 1980 and Almodóvar's first feature film *Pepi, Luci, Bom y Otras Chicas del Montón* (Pepi, Luci, Bom and All Those Other Girls). Shot on a low budget, it follows the adventures of the three characters of the title—Pepi, who wants revenge from the corrupt policeman who raped her; Luci, a masochistic housewife; and Bom, a lesbian punk-rock singer. His 1988 farcical film *Mujeres al borde de un ataque de nervios* (Women on the Verge of a Nervous Breakdown) got the attention of the international media and brought him to a much wider audience. (It has since been made into a Broadway musical.)

Todo sobre mi Madre (All About My Mother) won an Oscar in 2000 for best foreign-language film, and in 2003 *Hable con ella* (Talk to Her) won an Oscar for best original screenplay.

How did the Socialists advance the system of regional autonomy?

The 1978 Constitution established a quasi-federal state (see "How and why was the system of regional autonomy created?" in chapter 3). During the 1980s, 17 autonomous communities were established, each region with its own parliament and flag. The central government established in 1984 the *Fondo de Compensación Interterritorial* (Interterritorial Compensation Fund) to ensure an equitable financing of the regions, as their per capita levels of income vary considerably.

In 1989 the political class began to debate how to achieve the regional role intended by the Constitution for the Senate, the upper house of parliament. It was to operate along the lines of Germany's Bundesrat, which represents the 16 Länder (federal states) in order to increase regional participation in legislative activity and decision making. Nothing has been achieved since then on this issue. The Senate has 208 directly elected members and 58 appointed by the regions. Most of the 50 provinces elect four senators, without regard to population, and the Canary and Balearic Islands and the enclaves of Ceuta and Melilla on the North African coast elect between one and three senators. This allocation is heavily weighted in favor of small provinces, historically more conservative. The province of Madrid, for example, with a population of around six million, and Soria, with about 100,000, are each represented by four senators. Instead of making the Senate a truly regional chamber, the Socialists set up in 1994 the *Comisión General de las Comunidades Autónomas* (General Commission of Autonomous Communities), whose members are senators, representatives of the central government and of the regions.

The devolving of powers to the regions gradually reduced the central government's share of total public spending, from

72 percent in 1987 to 63 percent in 1992, and increased that of the regions from 12 percent to 23 percent over the same period (37 percent in 2011). The process of decentralization produced a surge in civil servants working for regional administrations (from 46,000 to 600,000 between 1982 and 1992 and up to 1.3 million in 2008). This was not offset by a commensurate reduction in the number of central government personnel. Most of the regional governments tended to replicate the organization and functions of the central government in their areas, which caused spending to rise considerably and recourse to debt to fund the expenditure. Two decades later, the regions' budget deficits and debt levels were a significant factor behind Spain's financial crisis and spooked the international debt markets.

As the process of devolution developed, so nationalist parties tied to a particular region assumed a greater importance in political life at the national level. This was particularly the case of the Catalan Convergència i Unió (CiU, Convergence and Union) and the Partido Nacionalista Vasco (PNV, Basque Nationalist Party), which assumed power-broker roles in the fourth government of Felipe González (1993–1996) and the first Popular Party (PP) government of José María Aznar (1996–2000), as the Socialists and the PP did not win an outright majority in national parliament in the 1993 and 1996 general elections. In return for supporting the Socialist government at the national level, the CiU won control of 15 percent of the levying of income tax in Catalonia, a measure that was also extended to all the other regions. In its own region, the CiU enjoyed a period of uncontested hegemony between 1981 and 2003, while the PNV dominated the Basque Country until the party split in 1987, which in turn required it to govern in coalition with the Socialists. The CiU and the pro-independence Esquerra Republicana de Catalunya (ERC, Catalan Republican Left) pushed for greater autonomy along the lines of that enjoyed by Basques, who have almost as much power over their own affairs as a German Land.

Why was a "dirty war" waged against the Basque terrorist group ETA?

When the Socialists took office at the end of 1982, following a failed coup in February 1981, they were caught between the fear of losing the support of the armed forces and the renewed killings by the Basque separatist organization ETA. The security apparatus they had inherited had changed little during the first years of democracy. The ETA killed 244 people between the approval of the democratic constitution in December 1978 and 1982. During this period, an extreme-right-wing group with close links to the security services calling itself the Batallón Vasco Español (BVE, Basque Spanish Battalion) conducted a dirty war against the ETA in which at least 10 people were killed, most notably José Miguel Benarán Ordeñana (nom de guerre, Argala), a leading ETA ideologue. Argala was directly involved in the December 20, 1973, assassination of Admiral Luis Carrero Blanco, Franco's prime minister and the man charged with continuing the regime after Franco's death. Instead of abandoning the dirty war, rogue elements, with the complicity of some senior members of a government that claimed to occupy the moral high ground, as it was untainted by Francoism, decided to continue it in order to force the ETA to lay down its arms. Another goal was to change the attitude of the French authorities toward the ETA and force them to collaborate with Spain by cracking down on the safe haven the group enjoyed in the French Basque Country. It was no coincidence that most of the 27 killings took place in southern France.

In October 1983, the Grupos Antiterroristas de Liberación (GAL, Anti-Terrorist Liberation Groups), death squads mainly made up of mercenaries, including Jean-Pierre Cherid, a far-right French activist involved in Argala's murder, and financed by secret government funds, kidnapped two 20-year-old ETA sympathizers, José Antonio Lasa Aróstegui and José Ignacio Zabala Artano, in Bayonne, France. (Cherid was killed in 1984 while activating a bomb.) The bodies of Lasa and Zabala, with gunshots in the heads and signs of having been tortured, were found in January 1985 in a quicklime grave in Alicante, Spain, 800 kilometers away. The judge at the postmortem attributed their deaths to "probably a settling of accounts between international gangsters" and shelved the case. The state had little interest in finding out the truth. A bold provincial pathologist, Antonio Bru Brotons, was suspicious of a cover-up and preserved the bones, which, in 1995, were identified as those of Lasa and Zabala. General Enrique Rodríguez Galindo of the Civil Guard and Julen Elgorriaga, the Socialist civil governor of Guipuzcoa, one of the Basque provinces, were subsequently convicted of involvement in the murders, along with two Civil Guard agents.

The GAL operated until 1987. Its victims (27 dead and 26 injured) were mainly suspected members of the ETA or linked to Basque nationalist activities, but some had no such links, particularly Segundo Marey, who was mistaken for an ETA activist and seized from his home in December 1983. When it became clear who he was, Marey was released along with a note from GAL stating that "each murder by the terrorists will have the necessary reply." In 1998, by which time the conservative Popular Party was in power, José Barrionuevo, the Socialist interior minister, Rafael Vera, his secretary of state for security, and Julián Sancristóbal, the civil governor of Vizcaya, were given prison sentences for their involvement in Marey's kidnapping.

Felipe González, the prime minister, denied that he was the person referred to in documents as Mr. X, the highest point in the hierarchy to sanction GAL. The closest González came to admitting any responsibility was when he declared that "democracy is defended in the sewers as well as in the salons." The GAL scandal caused immense damage to the Socialists. It showed that although the political transition to democracy had been completed, the security services had not learned or "internalized" the rules of democracy. Moreover, instead of forcing the ETA to disband, GAL's actions strengthened the group and won it support for its cause. The only positive aspect was that the media, by then completely free, did a fine job unearthing GAL, particularly the newspapers *Diario 16* and *El Mundo*. The justice system brought some of those responsible to account, largely due to the dogged investigations of Baltasar Garzón, the principal examining magistrate, who later gained international fame for issuing an international arrest warrant for the arrest of General Augusto Pinochet, the former Chilean president, for the alleged deaths and torture of Spanish citizens.

What were the corruption scandals that brought down the Socialists?

Felipe González won the election in 1993, though not with an absolute majority of seats in parliament. He promised *un cambio sobre el cambio* ("a change on top of the change"). This echoed the Socialists' successful slogan in 1982 of *por el cambio* ("time for change") and was in response to the growing disenchantment with his party over corruption and revelations over the GAL death squads after they had stopped operating. In a surprise move, González brought into parliament Baltasar Garzón, the examining magistrate who led the prosecution of GAL-related crimes. He was elected as an independent on the Socialists' ticket for Madrid and given a post in the government as the drug czar. Garzón felt he had been used by the Socialists to burnish the credentials of their anticorruption campaign, and he resigned after a year and resumed the GAL investigation.

Hardly a day passed, particularly during the fourth Socialist government, without some kind of scandal making newspaper headlines, making a mockery of their slogan of "one hundred years of honesty." A climate favorable to corruption and influence peddling was created by the lack of frequent alternation between political parties, the huge rise in public spending, the strong investment in public works, the devolution of power to the regions, and the increased costs of the functioning of political parties, together with an ineffective system of checks and balances. A new word appeared in the political jargon, *pelotazo*, which was defined in the dictionary of the Spanish Royal Academy in the 1990s as "a business of doubtful legality with which a lot of money is made quickly."

Among the figures brought down were Luis Roldán, the first civilian head of the Civil Guard, and Mariano Rubio, the governor of the Bank of Spain (the central bank). Roldán, who had been tipped to become interior minister, fled Spain in April 1994 after he was dismissed from his post and captured in Laos in February 1995. Over the course of seven years he had amassed a personal fortune of $40 million, largely from kickbacks on the construction of Civil Guard buildings. He was brought back to Spain and sentenced to 31 years in prison for bribery, falsification of documents, misuse of public funds, blackmail, and tax crimes. Rubio was briefly imprisoned as a result of his involvement in tax fraud and insider trading at Ibercorp bank, headed by Manuel de la Concha, the former president of the Madrid Stock Exchange. Rubio's case shocked Spaniards, because he headed the institution responsible for the well-being of the financial system. Another scandal involved Juan Guerra, the brother of Alfonso Guerra, the deputy prime minister, who was accused of influence peddling and becoming inexplicably rich.

Equally damaging for the Socialists was the Filesa scandal in the 1990s, in which 39 people were implicated in illegal financing of the party. This was done through payments for fictitious reports supposedly provided to businessmen by a consultancy firm in return for favors from the government. A typical example of this scam was a 17-page report produced for a supermarket chain at a cost of $250,000, 14 pages of which were photocopies of local council planning documents. In another scandal, the Socialists' sister trade union, the UGT, created a cooperative, Promoción Social de Viviendas (PSV), to build low-cost homes for thousands of its members. It suspended payments to suppliers and eventually declared bankruptcy.

Dubious accounting methods and speculative ventures unrelated to subsidized housing brought down the PSV. Nicolás Redondo, who had led the UGT since 1971 when it was illegal, was forced to resign.

Such scandals, however, were not confined to the Socialists. Gabriel Cañellas, the Popular Party's premier of the Balearic Islands, one of the 17 autonomous regions, was forced to resign in 1995 over irregularities in the building of a tunnel. Several PP politicians were involved in an illegal party-financing scheme in 1990 known as the Naseiro case. Various prominent businessmen, with political ambitions, were also involved in financial scandals, most notably Mario Conde, the chairman of Banesto, one of the country's largest and oldest banks. The Bank of Spain took over Banesto in 1993 after it discovered a multibillion-dollar black hole in its accounts and sacked the whole board. Conde was sentenced to 20 years in jail for fraud and embezzlement, and Banesto was sold to Banco Santander.

These and many other scandals were part of what became known as the *cultura del pelotazo* (the days of anything goes and get rich quick). Government and party officials were deeply reluctant to accept their political responsibilities in the scandals until magistrates had determined whether there were criminal charges to face. Officials were able to draw comfort from the snail's pace at which the legal system moves and the politicization of the judiciary. The members of the Consejo General del Poder Judicial (CGPJ, General Council of the Judiciary), the governing body of the judiciary, are nominated by parliament and the senate from the legal profession. As the Socialists were the majority party in both houses, most of the members of the CGPJ owed their allegiance to the party in power. Many of these scandals would not have happened or would have been detected early on if a vigorous separation of the powers of the executive, the legislative, and the judicial branches (checks and balances) had been in place. This problem still plagues Spain.

In parliament, there was a permanent state of confrontation between the Socialists and the Popular Party (PP), the main opposition, known as *crispación*. This hampered the political consensus needed for reforms and made political life tense. González was forced to hold an early election in March 1996 (it was not due until 1997) when his Catalan nationalist partners in the governing coalition refused to support his budget proposals in the autumn of 1995 for the following year. This was the first time a government had not completed its term in office since the restoration of democracy. The Socialists lost the election, but not by a wide margin. They won 37.6 percent of the votes and 141 of the 350 seats, compared to the PP's 38.8 percent and 156 seats. It was a sweet defeat for the Socialists and a bitter victory for the PP.

5

THE RETURN OF THE RIGHT, 1996–2004

How did the right reinvent itself and return to power in 1996 under the Popular Party?

The conservative Partido Popular's (PP, Popular Party) hunger for power, after 13 years of Socialist government, was amusingly depicted in a 1996 cartoon by El Roto in *El País*, the leading newspaper. It showed an archetypal Francoist and above him the words: "If the right does not win this time, I will no longer believe in democracy."

The PP grew out of the neo-Francoist Alianza Popular (AP, Popular Alliance) and formed in 1976 among seven former ministers (known collectively as the Magnificent Seven). The most notable of the ministers was Manuel Fraga, a former information and tourism minister (1962–1969) and interior minister in the first post-Franco government (1975–1976). The association of the AP (refounded as the PP as of 1989) with the Franco regime and hence with the victors of the Civil War was an electoral liability that imposed a "ceiling" on the votes it received in the 1982, 1986, and 1989 general elections. The PP did not receive more than 26 percent of votes until the 1993 election, by which time the party had been headed for four years by the much younger José María Aznar. The party experimented with two other leaders before Aznar, neither of whom lasted very long, and Fraga returned to try to restore order. The PP lost again in 1993, but by a much narrower margin—it captured 34.8 percent of the vote compared to the Socialists' 38.8 percent—and finally won in 1996 with 38.8 percent and 156 of the 350 seats in parliament.

The PP's victory strengthened the fledgling democracy. The transfer of power from Felipe González to Aznar was an historic occasion, as it was only the second time in 60 years in Spain that power passed from one elected party to another. The PP, however, was 20 seats short of an absolute majority, which forced Aznar to establish pacts with conservative Catalan and Basque nationalist parties in return for greater autonomy of these regions. The PP was and remains weak in the Basque Country and Catalonia, where the conservative nationalist parties take most of the center-right vote.

The PP captured the center ground, where most elections are won, by shedding its authoritarian image at home and abroad and becoming a more responsible opposition party. In 1986, AP had urged its supporters to abstain in the referendum on joining NATO, a crucial matter of foreign policy and one of natural support for a conservative party. The AP, however, put its own interests before those of the country, as it hoped the Socialists, who campaigned for a "yes" vote, would be defeated in the referendum and forced to hold an election. The presence of Christian Democrats with good democratic pedigrees in the PP, at first on an individual and not a group basis, helped to make the party more responsible and soften its image.

A turning point came in 1989 when the Partido de la Democracia Cristiana (PDC, the Christian Democrat Party) of Javier Rupérez dissolved and joined the PP. This marked the demise of Christian Democracy as an independent political force in Spain (and a small one at that), but enabled it to influence a broader movement that burnished the electoral chances of the Spanish right and helped turn the PP into a mainstream center-right European party. In 1991, the PP gained international respectability by becoming a full member of the European People's Party, the largest European-level political movement of the center right, and in 1993 it was admitted to the Christian Democrat International. By moderating its image, the PP managed to prevent the creation of an extreme-right party. As opposed to what happens on the left, where there are several parties, conservative voters in Spain have only one choice.

The PP managed to turn the tables on the Socialists, discredited by corruption scandals, and portray them as outdated. A much younger generation replaced the one that consolidated Spain's transition to democracy. Many of the PP's leaders were under 25 at the time of Franco's death in 1975. Their first political memories were of the Burgos trial of members of the Basque terrorist organization ETA and the assassination of Admiral Luis Carrero Blanco, Franco's prime minister, during the twilight years of the dictatorship, and their first experience of politics was as part of the opposition to the Socialists and not clandestine activities during the dictatorship. Their political mentors were Ronald Reagan and Margaret Thatcher, leaders of the conservative revolution during the 1980s.

Who is José María Aznar?

José María Aznar, prime minister of Spain between 1996 and 2004, was born in Madrid in 1953. His grandfather, Manuel, was a prominent journalist on Franco's side during the Civil War and later editor of *La Vanguardia*, the veteran newspaper based in Barcelona. As a teenager during the Franco dictatorship, Aznar was a member of a student union that supported the Falange. After graduating in law, he became a tax inspector and joined the neo-Francoist Popular Alliance (AP) in 1979. In 1982, he was elected to parliament representing the province of Ávila in the autonomous region of Castile and León, and in 1987 resigned his seat to head the AP's ticket for the elections in that traditionally conservative region. By then Spain had established a quasi-federal system.

He was premier of Castile and León until 1989, when he entered the national political arena as leader of the renamed Popular Party (PP), in place of Manuel Fraga, the founder of the AP, whose long association with the Franco regime made the party unelectable and riven by infighting and personality squabbles. Aznar broadened the PP's base by recruiting younger and unknown politicians to replace the Francoist old guard and exercising an iron control over the party. He turned the PP, in his words, into "a right-wing party that has nothing to be ashamed of and, unlike the UCD [the party that steered the transition to democracy], which had a bad conscience over the left, it does not have to ask forgiveness for anything, neither the Civil War nor Francoism." He created the FAES think tank in 1992, which has close links with conservative US think tanks and acts a laboratory of ideas for the PP.

Aznar came to power in 1996, without an absolute majority, under the slogan *Gana el centro* ("the center wins"). The church did not actively support the PP, but by calling on Catholics to vote for parties that defended the church's anti-abortion position (the Socialists had decriminalized abortion in 1985), it won the PP support, as Aznar had promised to annul any law that extended abortion. The appeal by bishops for ethical values to be restored to a body politic riddled with corruption echoed parts of the PP's manifesto. Aznar also won a sympathy vote when he narrowly escaped an attempt on his life in 1995 by the Basque terrorist group ETA, which 20 years after Franco's death was still waging a campaign of violence for an independent Basque nation.

The PP won an absolute majority in the election in 2000 (183 of the 350 seats in parliament). By then Aznar was a significant player on the European stage as the only center-right survivor among the leaders of the large EU countries, following social democrat Gerhard Schröder's ousting of chancellor Helmut Kohl in Germany and the New Labor candidate Tony Blair's defeat over conservative John Major in Great Britain. Despite apparent ideological differences, Aznar established a close relationship with Blair. They promoted the Lisbon Agenda in 2000 to make the European Union economy more competitive and knowledge based and together backed the US-led invasion of Iraq in 2003. A tougher line on Cuba, a former Spanish colony, was also part of Aznar's more pro-Atlanticist foreign policy. The European Union, on his initiative, established a common position on Cuba, which linked dialogue with the island's Communist authorities to moves on their part in favor of a democratic opening. This followed the summary execution by firing squad of three people who hijacked a ferry in an attempt to escape the country, and the roundup of 75 dissidents.

Aznar did not run for a third term in office in the 2004 election, as he could have done, and handed leadership of the PP to Mariano Rajoy. This was an unprecedented move in post-Franco politics.

How did the Popular Party meet the conditions to adopt the euro as Spain's currency?

When the Popular Party took office in 1996, Spain had recovered from its mild recession and the economy was growing again, but the country met none of the criteria for joining the Economic and Monetary Union (EMU) and using a common currency, the euro, as of 1999. Inflation, interest rates, the budget deficit, and public debt all breached the convergence requirements enshrined in the Maastricht Treaty of 1992 for setting up the euro zone. Public spending had risen from around 30 percent of the GDP in 1977 to 45 percent, and unemployment was 23 percent.

After a long period of isolation from mainstream Europe during the Franco regime, it was a matter of national pride that Spain was among the core countries of EMU and in the vanguard of a European movement. A constant during part of Spanish history has been the country's lack of synchronization with the rest of Europe. The desire to be in step explained the strong political support by all parties for EMU, as it did for European Economic Community (EEC) membership more than a decade earlier. This helped the PP in its appeal for sacrifices and made the road to the euro a lot less bumpy than it might otherwise have been. Civil servants agreed to a wage freeze, public spending was reduced, privatizations began on a larger scale than under the Socialists, and various structural measures were taken. By the spring of 1998, Spain had met the conditions: its budget deficit was less than the maximum allowance of 3 percent of the GDP (6.5 percent in 1995), public debt as a proportion of the GDP was on a downward path, and inflation was down to 2 percent from 4.5 percent in 1995. With it interest rates fell. The path was also eased by Spain's being the largest net recipient of EEC funds, much of which was used to greatly improve transport infrastructure. The macroeconomic stability ushered in another virtuous circle of high growth and job creation, similar to that experienced for almost a decade after Spain joined the EEC until the mild recession in 1993. The country's per capita income increased from 80 percent of the average of the 15 European Union countries in 1996 to 87 percent in 2004, and thanks to the creation of 1.8 million new jobs the unemployment rate dropped from 23 percent to 11.5 percent during this period.

Euro zone membership, however, deprived Spain of its former capacity to set interest rates and devalue its currency. Interest rates are set by the European Central Bank, not by member state central banks, and euro zone countries cannot devalue. The previous Socialist government devalued the peseta three times between 1992 and 1995. The loss of independence in these areas meant that when the Spanish economy entered a long period of recession as of 2008, as part of a meltdown of the whole euro zone, it could not use interest rates and a currency devaluation to restore competitiveness (see "What austerity measures were taken?" in chapter 6).

What role did privatization play in economic policy?

The Popular Party (PP) stepped up the pace of privatizations for ideological reasons and because it needed to maximize revenue to curb the budget deficit, lower the level of public debt, and meet European Union criteria on state ownership of industries. The great bulk of receipts came from the sale of stakes in Endesa, the dominant electricity group and the jewel in the state's crown, Repsol, the oil and gas group, Telefónica, the telecoms operator—all very profitable companies—and the airline Iberia. The chairmen of these and other privatized companies were businessmen close to the PP.

By 2001, when the PP was in its second term of office, the state's participation in the economy consisted of not much more than RTVE (two TV channels); Renfe, the railway company; the news agency Efe; Enresa (nuclear waste); the chain of *Parador* hotels and loss-making coal, defense, and shipbuilding companies. The government retained "golden shares" in the bank Argentaria, Telefónica, and Repsol in order to prevent hostile takeovers, which were later eliminated as a result of EU pressure.

What were the Popular Party's other main economic reforms?

The Popular Party's main economic achievement was macroeconomic stability, enabling Spain to be among the first wave of countries to use the euro and ushering in a 13-year period of sustained growth, much of which proved to be illusory, until 2008, when the economy took a nosedive. The government also undertook mild reforms in pensions and the labor market.

The 1997 labor legislation introduced a new permanent contract, with reduced severance payments. Spain's payments for workers with a permanent contract were among the most generous in Europe and a major factor behind employers' reluctance to hire workers on an indefinite basis. This made the labor market highly segmented between insiders on permanent contracts and outsiders on temporary contracts. The new contract was targeted at two groups: the population most exposed to unemployment (young adults, the long-term unemployed, and people above the age of 45) and workers on temporary contracts. It reduced severance payments in the event of an unjustified dismissal from 45 days' pay per year of service (up to a 42-month maximum) to 33 days per year (up to a 24-month maximum). This remained, nevertheless, above the European Union average. In 2001, under a further reform, the 33-day limit was applied more widely. The 1997 reform also moved further in the direction started by the Socialists in 1994 of clarifying when employers were justified in laying off workers and thus could pay lower severance payments of 20 days per year up to a 12-month maximum. The 1994 reform to broaden justifications had little effect because the labor courts continued to rule overwhelmingly in favor of workers.

The unemployment rate was halved to 11.5 percent during the PP's eight years in office, but massive job creation was largely due to the economic boom, and in particular the labor-intensive construction sector, and not to structural reforms. The dash to build hundreds of thousands of homes began after the 1998 Land Law, which massively increased the amount of land for development. The PP mistakenly thought this reform would lower land prices. It had the opposite effect. The number of housing starts rose from an average of 76,127 a year between 1990 and 1995 under the Socialists to 269,391 a year between 1996 and 2003 under the Popular Party. This concentration of activity in one sector produced a lopsided economy and created an enormous property bubble, which burst as of 2008 (see "What was the impact of the collapse of the property and construction sectors?" in chapter 6).

The long-term viability of the pay-as-you-go state pensions system was under pressure from an aging population, due to longer life expectancy (Spaniards, on average, live 82 years compared to 78 in the US), and the volatile unemployment rate. These two factors created the "pension trap" (where the elderly population is increasingly dependent on a shrinking number of people working). The Civil War caused a sharp fall in the birth rate and delayed the "baby boom" until 1960–1975, more than a decade later than in most other Western countries. The period for calculating the pension received was increased from the last eight years of contributions to the last 15 years, but the formula remained one of the most generous among developed countries.

The PP granted the 17 regional governments (created as a result of the 1978 Constitution, which established a quasi-federal system) powers to raise tax revenues in a bid to promote greater "co-responsibility" and make the regions less dependent on recourse to central government funding or the international debt markets. The two largest items funded by transfers from the central government to the regions were the devolved health and education systems. Until 1997, fiscal devolution was confined to the collection of the so-called ceded taxes (*tributos cedidos*), mainly on property, whose rates and conditions were nevertheless set by the central government. As of that year regional governments were allowed to set a component of the personal income tax rates applied to their region. The rates are divided into a state and a regional component. The regions were also authorized to vary income tax exemption thresholds. Between 1997 and 2001 the taxes over which regional governments had some capacity to change the base or the rate increased from about one-quarter to over one-half of current revenues. This reform, however, did not secure the fiscal discipline of regional governments, as limits were no longer set on the level of their debts and budget deficits, as had been the case during the European Monetary Union convergence process for the launch of the euro. As a result, regional governments raised funds on the financial markets to fund spending or obtained loans from banks, which contributed a decade later to Spain's ballooning budget deficits and financial crisis.

Why and how did Spain create multinational companies?

European Union membership as of 1986 made a significant number of companies, particularly state-run ones in oligopolistic sectors such as telecommunications (Telefónica), oil and natural gas (Repsol and Gas Natural), and electricity (Endesa)—all of which were to be privatized and become cash rich—expand abroad in order to offset the tougher competition on their home ground. The adoption of the euro in 1999 enabled companies to raise funds for their acquisitions at rates unimaginable just a few years previous. Outward direct investment soared from an annual average of $2.3 billion in 1985–1995 to $30.4 billion in 1995–2004, $94.3 billion in 2005–2007, and $40.8 billion in 2008–2011, according to the United Nations Conference on Trade and Development (UNCTAD).[1] The stock of Spain's outward investment at the end of 2011 was $640.3 billion and represented 42.5 percent of the GDP (3.0 percent in 1990). This was higher than Italy's investment abroad in absolute and GDP terms. Spain, along with South Korea and Taiwan, has produced the largest number of global multinationals among the countries that in the 1960s had not yet developed a solid industrial base (see table 5.1).

Latin America was a natural first choice for companies wishing to invest abroad. As well as cultural and linguistic affinities, there were factors that pulled companies to the region. Economic liberalization and privatization in Latin America opened up sectors that were hitherto off-limits, and the region's poor infrastructure was in constant need of development. Between 1993 and 2000, during the first phase of significant investment abroad, Telefónica, the banks Santander and BBVA, Repsol, Gas Natural, and the power companies Endesa, Iberdrola, and Unión Fenosa made acquisitions in the region. Investment in Latin America averaged $13.1 billion a year during this period. Only the United States, whose economy at that time was 12 times larger than Spain's and in whose backyard Latin America lies, invested more. By the early 2000s, Spanish companies had become the largest operators in

Table 5.1 Spanish Multinationals with the Largest Global Market Positions[1]

Company	Industry	Global Market Position
Ebro Puleva	Food processing	#1 producer of rice, and #2 of pasta
Grupo SOS	Food processing	#1 producer of olive oil
Viscofán	Food processing	#1 producer of artificial casings for the meat industry
Freixenet	Sparkling wine	#1 producer of sparkling wine
Tavex	Textiles	#1 producer of denim
Inditex	Clothing	#1 fashion retailer by sales
Pronovias	Clothing	#1 maker of bridal wear
Acerinox	Steel	#1 producer of stainless steel
Repsol	Energy	#3 privately owned shipper of liquefied gas
Roca	Sanitary equipment	#1 maker of sanitary equipment
Grupo Antolín	Automobile components	#1 producer of interior linings
Zanini	Automobile components	#1 producer of wheel trims
Gamesa	Machinery	#4 manufacturer of wind turbines
Indo	Optical equipment	#3 manufacturer of lenses
Mondragón	Diversified	#1 worker-owned cooperative group
Iberdrola	Electricity	#1 wind farm operator
Grupo Ferrovial	Infrastructure	#7 developer & manager of transportation infrastructure[2]
ACS/Hochtief	Infrastructure	#1 developer & manager of transportation infrastructure[2]

(Continued)

Table 5.1 (Continued)

Company	Industry	Global Market Position
Acciona	Infrastructure, renewable energy, and water	#6 in wind energy and #7 in renewables
Abertis	Infrastructure	#3 developer & manager of transportation infrastructure[2]
Telefónica	Telecom	#5 telecom operator by total customers
Santander	Banking	#4 most valuable bank brand, largest bank by market capitalization in the euro zone, and #1 franchise in Latin America
Prosegur	Security	#3 company by sales
Sol Meliá	Hotels	#1 holiday hotel chain by number of beds
Real Madrid	Sports	#1 soccer club by revenue

(1) 2011 or latest available.

(2) Ranked by number of road, bridge, tunnel, rail, port, and airport concessions over $50 million investment value put under construction or operation as of October 1, 2012.

Source: Compiled by William Chislett, Esteban García-Canal, and Mauro F. Guillén from Interbrand, Public Works Financing, BrandFinance, Bloomberg New Energy Finance, the Spanish Business Council for Competitiveness, and company reports.

telecommunications, electricity, water, and financial services in the region, and the profits generated there were making a significant contribution to their overall earnings. Santander's rise from a local note-issuing bank in the 19th century in the northern province of the same name to its position as the euro zone's leading retail bank (and the largest by market capitalization), with the biggest franchise in Latin America, is particularly remarkable. The bank has more than 100 million clients worldwide and generates a much bigger slice of its profits in Brazil than in Spain. The other large Spanish bank, BBVA, earns more in Mexico than at home.

The shift away from Latin America and into Europe, the United States, and Asia began in the early 2000s, after Argentina's financial meltdown, which hit Spanish banks and companies located there. The move was marked by several emblematic investments, including Telefónica's $32.2 billion purchase of the O_2 mobile telephony operator in the United Kingdom, Germany, and Ireland; a stake in China Netcom; Santander's $15.6 billion acquisition of the UK bank Abbey; and BBVA's acquisition of two small banks in California and Texas. In 2000 the *Financial Times'* list of the world's 500 biggest companies by market capitalization included only eight from Spain; by 2008 the figure had risen to 14 (it was down to six in the 2012 ranking).

The acquisitions and diversification enabled Spain's leading companies to offset the severe crisis in their domestic market between 2008 and 2013. More than 60 percent of the revenues of the companies that comprise the Ibex-35, the blue-chip index of the Madrid Stock Exchange, are generated abroad. Inditex, the owner of the Zara clothes chain, which opened its first shop in Galicia in 1975 and in less than 40 years became the world's largest clothes retailer by sales with more than 6,000 stores in 86 countries, including 400 in China, generates more than 70 percent of its revenues internationally. Two notable technology companies are Grifols (health care) and Abengoa (alternative energy and environmental services), both of them listed on Nasdaq.

How did Spain cope with the influx of immigrants?

Immigrants began to arrive in significant numbers during the Popular Party's eight-year government. When General Franco died in 1975 Spain had 165,000 foreign inhabitants. In 1995 there were more than 900,000, by 2005 the number had risen to 3.7 million, and in 2012 there were 5.7 million. Spain went from being a net exporter of people—in the 1950s and 1960s several million emigrated to Latin America and northern Europe—to the largest recipient of immigrants in the European Union in the shortest period. As a proportion of the total population, the foreigners' share has risen from 0.4 percent in 1975 to more than 12 percent, the highest figure among the large European countries.

As with so many other changes in Spain, the influx of immigrants occurred quickly. It was also a new phenomenon in a country that was intolerant for centuries and drove its citizens abroad for political, religious, or economic reasons. According to the historian Henry Kamen, between 1492, with the massive expulsion of Jews and Muslims, and 1975 around three million Spaniards left the country under political or economic pressure, without counting the very many others who formed part of a regular process of emigration, particularly during the 1960s.[2]

Immigrants were lured by an economy that was rapidly expanding and creating jobs, particularly in the construction sector. At the peak of the economic boom in 2007 more than half of the 3.3 million non-EU immigrants worked in the construction sector. Until then the country was a comparatively ethnically homogeneous society. The largest number of immigrants initially were Moroccans, many of whom entered Spain illegally by crossing the treacherous Straits of Gibraltar in rickety boats at great risk to their lives. Not only is Spain close to Morocco—at the nearest point, only 14 kilometers separates the two countries—but Spain's average per capita income is 10 times higher than Morocco's $3,000. Spain loomed like an "El Dorado" for impoverished Moroccans. After Rumania joined the European Union in 2004, it overtook Morocco as the largest foreign community in Spain (897,000 at the beginning of 2012, compared to 788,000 Moroccans), as EU citizens enjoy the right of free movement within the Union, unlike Moroccans and other non-EU citizens who need work and residency permits to work legally in Spain. In 2001, there were fewer than 60,000 Rumanians in Spain. Other large foreign communities are from the United Kingdom (mainly retirees) and from Ecuador and Colombia. More than half of foreigners in Spain are from non-EU countries.

The influx of immigrants was a consequence of, and then a contributor to, Spain's prosperity. In 2003, Spain received one in every three immigrants arriving in the European Union. Were it not for immigrants, Spain would not have been able to harvest its strawberries in Huelva, collect its pears in Lérida, find enough people to work in intensive agriculture in sweltering heat in plastic greenhouses in Almeria, sustain its construction boom, maintain hotels in tourist areas, and find nannies to look after children and people to care for the elderly in their homes. Immigrants were responsible for half of Spain's average annual GDP growth of 3.1 percent between 2001 and 2005, compared with 12 percent of the 4.1 percent growth between 1996 and 2000, according to a report by the Spanish government.[3] Immigrants also made Spain's notoriously rigid labor market more flexible, as they were less demanding than native workers, and they reversed the previously projected decline in the country's population, caused by the fall in the fertility rate (from 2.8 children in 1978 to 1.2 in 2000 and below the replacement rate of 2.1 needed to maintain a stable population). Close to two-thirds of the 6 million increase in the population between 2001 and 2011, Spain's largest-ever rise in a 10-year period, was due to the influx of immigrants and the higher fertility rate of female immigrants than that of Spanish women.

Immigrants have also changed Spain's religious map. From being an almost exclusively Catholic country, there were in 2012 around 1.4 million Muslims, 1.2 million Protestants/evangelicals, 500,000 members of Orthodox churches (Rumania, Bulgaria, and Russia), 125,000 Jehovah's Witnesses, and 48,000 Jews, according to the Registry of Religious Institutions.

Immigrants did not take away jobs from Spaniards, as most of them arrived during the country's economic boom and did the menial work that Spaniards were no longer willing to do. To some extent this explained why Spaniards were remarkably tolerant of immigrants. There was no backlash against them, nor the creation of an anti-immigrant and xenophobic party along the lines of France's or Britain's National Front. The only really serious anti-immigrant riots were at El Ejido in Almería in 2000, where hundreds of North Africans are employed in the plastic hothouses that produce Europe's winter vegetables in sweltering heat. The building of new mosques, particularly in urban centers, has, however, been controversial, and some were built on the outskirts of towns and cities because of popular opposition.

The labor force increased significantly between 1998 and 2007, and at the same time, the unemployment rate was more than halved to 8 percent. This was a remarkable achievement, but it was not sustainable. When the economy went into recession as of 2009, immigrants bore a large part of the surge in unemployment, as many of them were on temporary contracts in the construction sector and were the first to lose their jobs when the property bubble burst. The jobless rate among immigrants (more than 35 percent in 2013) is much higher than the national average (more than 25 percent in 2013). As a result, they began to return home in significant numbers as of 2010, at the same time as tens of thousands of Spaniards started to emigrate again, but in a different phenomenon from that of the 1960s, when unskilled workers moved to northern Europe. This time those emigrating were skilled and included engineers and doctors. Since 2011, for the first time in 30 years, the number of people emigrating (Spaniards seeking work abroad and foreigners returning home) has exceeded the number arriving in Spain, and many Spaniards have had no option but to do the menial jobs that had been earlier ceded to immigrants, such as harvesting grapes.

How did the Popular Party try to eradicate the Basque terrorist group ETA?

The Basque terrorist organization ETA's attempt to kill José María Aznar in 1995 with a car bomb, a year before he became prime minister, hardened the stance of his Popular Party (PP) toward the group. The ETA had been fighting for an independent Basque socialist state formed from provinces in northern Spain and the southwest of France for more than 30 years.

The PP was more ideologically intolerant of Basque nationalism than the social democrats of the previous Socialist government and more disposed to eradicate the ETA by police and not political means. By the time the PP assumed power, the ETA had killed 747 people, 374 of them during the preceding 13 years of Socialist rule (an annual average of 29). Arrests of suspected ETA members and imprisonments rose considerably after the PP took office, partly due to increased cooperation with neighboring France, which made that country a less secure safe haven for ETA activists. The number of ETA killings dropped from 15 in 1995 to five in 1996. The murder in July 1997 of Miguel Ángel Blanco, a PP town councilor in the Basque Country, marked a turning point and sent a wave of revulsion through Spain, bringing six million people onto the streets against the ETA. Blanco was killed after the government refused to meet the ETA's 48-hour ultimatum to move ETA prisoners closer to the Basque provinces.

The government also began to look more closely at the links between the ETA and its political allies, known collectively as the *izquierda abertzale* (patriotic left). In December 1997, 23 members of Herri Batasuna (HB) were jailed for seven years for collaborating with the ETA. The case centered on a video featuring armed activists, which the ETA's mouthpiece had tried to show during the 1996 general election campaign. This was the first time any members of the HB, founded in 1978, were imprisoned for cooperating with the ETA. The Basque newspaper *Egin*, in a separate case, was closed down.

In September 1998 a major political realignment took place in the Basque Country with the signing of the Estella Pact by all Basque nationalist parties, in which they agreed to intensify the nation-building process by peaceful means. This further polarized the region by dividing it into nationalists and non-nationalists. Until then the political divide had been on the basis of those who supported the institutional status quo, including the center-right Partido Nacionalista Vasco (PNV, Basque Nationalist Party), the region's main nationalist political force, although many of its supporters voted against or abstained in the national referendum on the 1978 Constitution, and nationalists, chiefly the more radically pro-independence HB. The PNV's more open backing of self-determination put it at odds with the minority PP government, which it supported in the national parliament in Madrid.

The ETA declared its first "indefinite" cease-fire and the HB rebranded itself under the name Euskal Herritarrok (EH, the Basque for "We, the Basque citizens") in a bid to gain wider support. It won 18 percent of the votes in the October 1998 election for the Basque parliament, making it the third-largest party after the PNV and the PP. The PNV, having previously formed coalition governments with the Basque Socialist party, joined forces with the more radical EH. The government had some direct contacts with the ETA, but nothing came of the meetings. The ETA wanted a peace deal that included a referendum on independence—a demand the PP categorically ruled out. In November 1999, the ETA ended its 14-month cease-fire and resumed killing (murdering 46 people between 2000 and 2004, when the Socialists returned to power).

Why did Spain support the US-led invasion of Iraq in 2003?

After Aznar won a second term in office in 2000 with an absolute majority, which gave him a freer hand than he had in his first minority government, he aspired to a Spanish equivalent of the United Kingdom's "special" relationship with Washington. This shift in foreign policy broke with the post-Franco, essentially European-focused and consensus-based policy, largely dictated by the determination among the whole political class to join the European Union.

Aznar had become disillusioned with the economic policies of France and Germany for not being sufficiently market friendly. He saw a closer relationship with Washington as a counterweight to the Franco-German dominance of the European Union. He viewed it as a way to further Spain's economic and business interests in the United States, particularly among the rapidly growing Hispanic community, which is larger than Spain's population, and raise the country's profile on the global stage. And it would not be a one-way street: closer ties would encourage greater direct investment in Spain by US companies. Aznar had his eyes set on Spain's becoming a member of an enlarged G-8, the forum for eight of the world's largest economies. He also aspired to place the Spanish economy, which thanks to the spectacular growth in the 1990s became at one point the eighth-largest economy in the developed world, more within the camp of the Anglo-Saxon model of capitalism and away from the social democratic version pursued by the Socialists in Spain. In this respect, he and Tony Blair, Britain's prime minister, worked closely on the Lisbon Agenda to make the EU economy more competitive.

The opportunity to forge closer political and economic relations with Washington came after the terrorist attacks on September 11, 2001, against the World Trade Center in New York. This galvanized the connection between Aznar and President George W.

Bush. Both men were ideologically close, and Aznar had himself been the victim of a terrorist bomb attack by the Basque terrorist group ETA in 1995. When Bush made Madrid his stopping-off point on his first presidential visit to Europe, Aznar spoke at great length to him about terrorism. The two men agreed on the need for a global war on terrorism. In 2003, Spain became a non-permanent member of the United Nations Security Council, by which time Aznar was the United States' most solid European ally along with Blair. Aznar was the main instigator of the article published in the *Wall Street Journal* in January 2003, signed by the prime ministers of eight European countries, which said that "the transatlantic relation must not fall victim to the constant attempts of the Iraqi regime to threaten world security." Aznar unsuccessfully tried to persuade Mexico and Chile, also non-permanent members of the Security Council, to back a UN resolution authorizing the use of force in Iraq because of Saddam Hussein's alleged stockpiling of weapons of mass destruction. At the height of Madrid's support for Washington, the Spanish government ran a marketing campaign in the United States with the tagline: "Your friend in Europe."

Spain joined the "coalition of the willing," symbolized by the photograph of Bush, Blair, and Aznar at their summit in the Azores in March 2003, shortly before the invasion of Iraq. Aznar justified his participation on the grounds that "Spain can no longer be in the same corner as the countries which do not count, do not serve and do not decide. In order to place our country among the most important ones in the world when the world is threatened, Spain must assume its responsibilities." In his memoirs, published in 2004, Aznar explained the decision further: "In the last 200 years, our country had not assumed international responsibilities. Since the disaster of the Napoleonic invasion, Spain was expelled from European politics at the Congress of Vienna in 1815. Since then, save one or two exceptions, Spain has turned in on itself."[4] In another book, Aznar said, "Spain was at the Azores because it could not participate in the Normandy landing (1944), which is where we should have been."[5]

Aznar, however, did not contribute combat troops to Iraq, as this would have been too controversial in a country that was overwhelmingly against the invasion—including a large segment of his own party and the Catholic Church. According to a poll conducted by the Elcano Royal Institute, a Madrid-based think tank, in the month before the invasion of Iraq, 64 percent of Spaniards opposed any kind of military intervention in Iraq, 27 percent would support it only if it had the backing of the United Nations, and only 2 percent approved the use of force with or without a resolution. Aznar sent 1,300 troops for peace-keeping and postwar reconstruction. Aznar's high-handed manner turned foreign policy into a battleground with the Socialists, whose very first decision, after winning the election in March 2004, was to bring home the troops from Iraq.

Why did Islamic terrorists bomb trains in Madrid on the eve of the 2004 general election?

On March 11, 2004, as thousands of commuters made their way to work, 10 bombs packed with nails on four trains heading to Madrid's Atocha station exploded, killing 192 people and injuring 1,800 others. It was the most devastating Islamist terrorist attack in Europe since the Lockerbie explosion in 1988 that killed 258 people on a Pan Am flight in Scotland.

The blasts of 11-M, as the events are known, occurred three days before a general election and were perpetrated by a cell affiliated with al Qaeda in retaliation for Spain's support of the war with Iraq. The cell consisted of a group of young immigrant men from North Africa, assisted by Spanish small-time criminals who provided the dynamite, one of whom was a 16-year-old boy known as *El Gitanillo* (the little gypsy). According to prosecutors at the trial of some of the plotters, the terrorists were influenced by a tract on an al Qaeda–affiliated website that called for attacks on Spain. The tract called for "two or three attacks...to exploit the coming general elections in Spain," saying that they would ensure the "victory of the

Socialist party and the withdrawal of Spanish forces [from Iraq]." The Socialists' candidate, José Luis Rodríguez Zapatero, pledged in March 2003 (one year before 11-M) to withdraw Spain's troops from Iraq if his party returned to power at the next election, which it did (see "Did the Socialists return to power because of the Islamic terrorist attack"? in chapter 6).

The attack on the trains was not the first one by Islamic terrorists in Spain. In April 1985, a bomb planted in a restaurant near Madrid and frequented by military personnel from the nearby US air base at Torrejón killed 18 people. Investigations after the attack in New York on September 11, 2001, revealed that some of those involved had visited Spain to obtain false documents and other materials. Ayman Al Zawahiri, a close associate of Osama bin Laden, said a month after 9–11 that al-Andalus, the Arabic name that Muslim conquerors gave to the Iberian Peninsula until they were conquered by Christian armies in 1492, would one day revert to Islamic rule. In May 2003, a suicide bomb attack on the Casa de España (the House of Spain) social center in Casablanca, Morocco, killed 45 people.

Other factors that put Spain on the jihadist map were its proximity to North Africa and the large Muslim immigrant community in the country, a tiny part of which was disaffected and vulnerable to joining the Islamic fundamentalist cause. Spaniards' opposition to the war was also very high at 90 percent, according to opinion polls, and brought millions of people into the streets. Spain was thus viewed by jihadists as the best place for a successful attack. European security services at the time considered London a more likely target than Madrid for a terrorist attack. This was because Britain was Washington's closest ally in the Iraq war.

The government was quick to pin the blame for the blasts on the Basque terrorist group ETA, against whom the PP had taken a hard line. Aznar phoned newspaper editors to this effect, and Spanish ambassadors were told to push the ETA line. Initially, it was natural for the government to attribute the attack to the ETA, as the group had been waging a campaign of violence for more than 30 years. It had unsuccessfully targeted Madrid railway stations, and two of its activists had been caught a month before 11-M transporting half a ton of explosives to the Spanish capital. However, as evidence began to be found, including a bag with explosives that had failed to detonate, a van containing seven detonators, and a tape of recitations of the Koran, three Moroccans were arrested. It was clear that the ETA was not responsible. The government was slow to release this and other information to the public in the final run-up to the election, laying itself open to accusations of manipulating the evidence for the PP's electoral benefit. On the eve of voting a videocassette was found near the central Madrid mosque, on which an Al Qaeda spokesman claimed responsibility for the bombings. Thousands of people, mobilized by text messages and the Internet, protested outside the PP's headquarters in Madrid, in defiance of the electoral law banning political activities the day before the election.

The 11-M Commission set up by the Socialists after they won the election eliminated any suspicion of involvement by the ETA and found that the Aznar government had manipulated information for electoral purposes. It also affirmed that the government had underestimated the Islamic terrorist threat to Spain. All parties except the PP approved the conclusions. Nevertheless, PP supporters continued to peddle conspiracy theories for several years. Victims' associations were also divided and politicized the tragedy. The Asociación 11-M Afectados por el Terrorismo (11-M Association of those Affected by Terrorism), led by Pilar Manjón, the mother of one of the victims, was highly critical of the PP government, while the much older Asociación de Víctimas del Terrorismo, founded in 1981 as a result of the ETA's killings, took a hard stance against the Socialists. The 11-M victims are commemorated in a towering glass memorial monument at Atocha station with the names of the 192 victims, around one-quarter of whom were immigrants working in the country.

6

THE SOCIALISTS STRIKE BACK, 2004–2011

Did the Socialists return to power because of the Islamic terrorist attack?

The Socialists under José Luis Rodríguez Zapatero won the election on March 14, 2004, three days after the Islamic terrorist attacks that killed 192 people in Madrid. They captured 11 million votes compared to 9.7 million by the Popular Party (PP), but they were 12 parliamentary seats short of an absolute majority and had to rely on support from the Communist Izquierda Unida (IU, United Left) and Esquerra Republicana de Catalunya (ERC, Catalan Republican Left).

The PP and the Socialists interpreted the results in very different ways and continued to do so for several years. The PP said that the attack revived antiwar feelings over its support for the invasion of Iraq, a move that was overwhelmingly opposed by Spaniards. They also laid blame on the way in which these feelings were channeled by the left and media opposed to the war. The party regarded Zapatero as an "accidental" prime minister.

The Socialists claimed they would have won the election regardless, and more so because of the PP's attempts to pin the blame for the attack on the Basque terrorist group ETA, a piece of deceit that backfired. Zapatero had pledged one year before the attacks to withdraw Spanish troops from Iraq if he won

the election, and his identity politics (social reforms and connection with minority groups) also gained him support. Had
the ETA been responsible for the blasts, the PP would most
probably have won the election. The attacks mobilized voters
who might otherwise have abstained or were undecided. Voter
turnout was 77 percent, the third highest since the return of
democracy in 1977. A low voter turnout in Spain tends to benefit the right more than the left, as the former is generally more
united around a single party (the PP) while the left is splintered
into several parties, including the Socialists and IU. According
to a poll after the election by the government-funded Center
for Sociological Research, 22 percent (some 1.6 million voters)
said the attack had influenced their decision and motivated
them to vote.

The Socialists' victory and the rapid withdrawal of Spanish
troops from Iraq were interpreted in international, right-wing
political and media circles and in parts of the PP as a capitulation to terrorism. According to this misguided view, bin Laden
was the winner of the election and not Zapatero. The historian
Charles Powell said this was like saying the 1980 US presidential election was won by Iran's Ayatollah Ruhollah Khomeini
and not Ronald Reagan, who beat Jimmy Carter after the latter
came to political grief at the hands of the Iranian revolutionary
leader over a failed mission to rescue Americans taken hos-
tage.[1] Spaniards were no strangers to terrorism. They had long
resisted the demands of the Basque group ETA—11 million
people out of a population of 42 million protested the 11-M
bombings before they knew for certain who was responsible—
and they had equally vociferously declared their opposition to
their government's support for the war with Iraq.

Who is José Luis Rodríguez Zapatero?

José Luis Rodríguez Zapatero was virtually unknown among
the majority of Spaniards before he became the head of the
Socialist Party in July 2000, after the resignation of Joaquín

Almunia and the party's defeat by the conservative Popular Party in the election that year. Zapatero was born in 1960 in Valladolid in the predominantly conservative region of Castile and León. His paternal grandfather, a Republican captain, was executed by General Franco's troops for refusing to join the rebel side during the Civil War. He wrote his will, in which he described his creed as a "love for peace, for good and for improving the living conditions of the lower classes," by hand 24 hours before facing a firing squad. This family tragedy probably influenced Zapatero's approach to the Civil War and led his government to approve the controversial Historical Memory Law in 2007 (see the question in this chapter). Zapatero's maternal grandfather, the one he knew, fought on Franco's side, something Zapatero carefully underplayed.

He headed the Socialist youth organization in the province of León and after studying and teaching law at the city's university became the youngest member of the national parliament in Madrid at the age of 26. He ran for the national leadership of the party after founding a faction called Nueva Vía (New Way), a name with echoes of the Third Way of Tony Blair, the United Kingdom's prime minister, and Neue Mitte (New Center) of Germany's social democrat chancellor, Gerhard Schröder. Zapatero was the dark-horse candidate running against three more experienced politicians. Zapatero's lack of experience and look earned him the nickname "Bambi" from Alfonso Guerra, a former Socialist deputy prime minister (1982–1991). Yet as the least associated with previous Socialist administrations and the youngest of the candidates, his message of the need to renew and rejuvenate a party that was discredited at the end of its fourth term in office (1993–1996) resonated at the primary election. He narrowly won, gaining 414 votes out of 995, nine more than his nearest rival.

Zapatero's political philosophy draws on the theories of freedom and "non-denomination" offered by Princeton academic Philip Pettit in his 1997 book *Republicanism*. Pettit defined what he calls "civil republicanism" as respect for "all

communities, identities, collectives and ideas as they all contribute to avoiding domination by some over others." Zapatero
passed a raft of socially progressive legislation and altered the
balance with the powerful Catholic Church in Spain (see the
next two questions).

In foreign policy, Zapatero gained a reputation before he took
office as anti-American, after he conspicuously refused to stand
up when the American flag passed by during the National Day
military parade in Madrid on October 12, 2003. He did so in
protest at the US-led war with Iraq. His attempts to soften the
European Union's common policy of linking relations with the
Communist regime in Cuba with Havana's progress in achieving democracy also antagonized Washington. Washington
was upset, too, by Zapatero's close relations with Venezuela's
avowedly anti-American president, Hugo Chávez. After the
United States' cozy relationship with the former Spanish prime
minister, José María Aznar, who supported the war with Iraq,
George W. Bush froze out Zapatero for being a disloyal ally. In
a pointed snub to Zapatero, Aznar was invited to the White
House in 2004, after he left office, while Zapatero had to wait
five years, until Bush was replaced by Barack Obama, before
he received an invitation. The tensions with Washington, however, did not prevent Zapatero from increasing to 1,500 the
number of Spanish peacekeeping troops in Afghanistan. He
regarded this as a justifiable cause as, unlike the war with Iraq,
the military intervention in Afghanistan had the blessing of the
United Nations.

How did Spain become one of the most socially progressive countries?

Spain made considerable progress in the first 30 years after
the end of the Franco dictatorship in political and economic
modernization, but less so in the field of social reform. As the
country that coined the word *machismo*, Spain was still excessively male-dominated and chauvinistic, and this culture was

deeply ingrained in society. There had been a sexual revolution with the introduction of contraceptives, but mentalities had changed little, particularly among older generations.

Zapatero immediately established his feminist credentials by forming the first cabinet in Spanish history equally divided between male and female ministers, one of whom, María Teresa Fernández de la Vega, was the first woman to be deputy prime minister. An equality law required political parties to allot 40 percent of their candidate lists to women and large companies (with over 250 employees) to give 40 percent of the seats on their boards to women, both of which have yet to be fulfilled. A domestic violence law came into force in 2005 to protect victims, support their recovery from acts of violence, and impose heavy penalties on perpetrators. In the eight years before Zapatero became prime minister, some 600 women died because of gender violence. The number of women who die at home at the hands of their partners dropped to 46 in 2012, the lowest yearly figure in more than a decade. Paternity leave was given greater recognition and maternity leave conditions improved. Stem-cell research was encouraged.

The most controversial reform was the legalization in 2005 of marriage between same-sex couples. Only three other countries in the world at that time had taken this step—Holland, Belgium, and Canada. Gay couples were also allowed to adopt children. The conservative Popular Party appealed against the law to the Constitutional Court and pressed for the word "union" to replace that of marriage, a term it said was applicable only to heterosexual couples. The court upheld the law in November 2012 after seven years of deliberations.

In abortion, a termination was allowed up to the 14th week of gestation and up to 22 weeks in the case of rape, fetal abnormality, or risk to the mother's health, and up to the moment of birth if the unborn child had a serious or incurable illness (as determined by a medical committee).

The new divorce law in 2005 introduced a fast-track system known as *divorcio exprés* under which couples no longer had to be separated for a year prior to legal proceedings and there was no requirement to attribute responsibility for the failure of the marriage. The number of divorces rose 73 percent in the first year after the law was introduced.

Lastly, public support for people unable to lead independent lives for reasons of illness, disability, or age was provided by the dependent care law. Until then the burden of caring for these people fell disproportionately on family members, particularly mothers, daughters, or wives who were deprived of or limited in their ability to earn a living, as they were expected to look after ailing relatives for nothing or pay for a caregiver. According to a study by the ministry of social affairs, some 1.1 million elderly people and/or persons with severe disabilities could not attend to their basic daily needs. Of this number, 73 percent were over 65 years old. Furthermore, some 1.6 million persons needed some type of support for certain activities of daily life. In total, this amounted to 2.7 million people, 6.4 percent of the Spanish population.

The government also committed itself to caring more for the poor in developing countries by setting itself the ambitious goal of assigning 0.7 percent of the GDP to official development assistance (ODA) every year as of 2012, and so become one of the first developed nations to reach the figure recommended by the United Nations. In 2011, the amount allocated represented only 0.3 percent because of the country's recession.

How did the Catholic Church react to the reforms?

The same-sex-marriage, divorce, and abortion laws, which put Spain in the social vanguard, set the Socialists on a collision course with the Catholic Church. Cardinal Antonio Rouco Varela, the archbishop of Madrid, accused José Luis Rodríguez Zapatero, the prime minister, of turning Spain into "Sodom and Gomorrah." The Spanish Bishops' Conference said the same-sex marriage law "introduced a dangerous and disruptive element into the institution of marriage, and thereby into our just social order." Some Popular Party (PP) mayors refused to marry same-sex couples, and a demonstration in Madrid, organized by the church and the PP to "defend the family," drew several hundred thousand protesters.

Zapatero also abolished the practice of displaying religious symbols in public places, which was seen as contrary to the non-confessional state established by the 1978 Constitution. He likewise shelved a law on compulsory religious instruction in public schools, said that religion was no longer an academic subject and that study of it could not count toward the school leaving certificate, and curtailed subsidies to *centros concertados*, which are private schools mainly run by the church. Zapatero added a course to the school curriculum called *Educación para la Ciudadanía* (Education for Citizenship) to promote civic and human values. The church and the PP said this course, which increasingly existed in other countries, was doctrinal and political and infringed upon parents' right to choose the education they wanted for their children. From being a bastion of Catholicism, Spain sought to become one of the most secular countries. The Vatican accused the Socialists of "lay fundamentalism and agnostic totalitarianism."

Despite the tense relations between the Socialists and the church, the two sides agreed to a new funding system. As of 2007, the state stopped paying an annual allowance to the church. To compensate for this loss, the government increased the amount of voluntary donations to the church that taxpayers were allowed to claim on their yearly tax declaration from 0.52 to 0.7 percent. According to the 1979 agreement between Spain and the Vatican, the church was slated to be self-financing as of the 1990s, but this had still not happened in 2013.

What was the Law of Historical Memory?

The Pacto de Olvido (literally, the Pact of Forgetting) was a tacit agreement among the whole spectrum of political parties during the transition to democracy to not open up the wounds of the Civil War and the dictatorship or use the past for political purposes. Civil society was complicit in this approach. There was nothing approaching truth and reconciliation commissions or war-crimes trials.[2] The pact was institutionalized by the 1977 Amnesty Law, which covered all crimes of a political nature committed prior to December 1976. This approach, however, did not prevent a deluge of history books, novels, memoirs, and films on the Civil War.

The pact began to be chipped away in the 1990s. The Socialists feared losing to the conservative Popular Party (PP) in the 1993 election and in their campaign used the PP's Francoist origins to insinuate that democracy was at risk. After the PP was returned to power in 2000 with an absolute majority for the first time, parliament received a range of initiatives from the left and the Basque and Catalan nationalist parties to condemn the Civil War and the Franco regime. The past became a political issue. Although the PP felt there was no need to recover the memory of the past, it signed a common declaration condemning the Civil War and the dictatorship in the hope that this would put a stop to the parliamentary initiatives for specific measures to be adopted. It did not. José Luis Rodríguez Zapatero, the Socialist leader as of 2000, made the "recovery of historical memory" part of his electoral program in the 2004 election and won. By then there was also considerable pressure from grassroots organizations, particularly the Association for the Recovery of Historical Memory.

The Law of Historical Memory, bitterly opposed by the PP, was passed in the autumn of 2007. Where there had been consensus not to instrumentalize the past politically, or open up old wounds or create new ones, there was now division. The Socialist leadership, with no direct memories or experience of the Civil War or the Franco regime, unlike the leadership when the party was in power between 1983 and 1996, felt the time had come to honor all the victims of the conflict and the dictatorship. It believed the country's democracy was sufficiently mature and consolidated to handle the unfinished business of the transition. Spain was the only case of a country that had moved to democracy in the 20th century not to have undertaken any kind of self-examination at state level of the crimes committed by the dictatorship that preceded democracy. The shift in attitudes was partly prompted by the attempt in 1998 by Baltazar Garzón, a maverick investigative magistrate and something of a self-publicist, to extradite Chile's former dictator, Augusto Pinochet, a self-confessed admirer of Franco, for the deaths and alleged torture of several Spanish citizens. Garzón's move laid Spain open to the charge of hypocrisy, since no official from the dictatorship had been held to account.

The Franco regime had only remembered those who died fighting for its cause; in 1940 it decreed the compiling of a list of killings committed by Republican loyalists, known as the *Causa General* (General Cause). The Law of Historical Memory declared illegitimate the military tribunals that condemned people to prison or death; banned public symbols commemorating, Franco and his allies; urged the church, which called Franco's uprising a "crusade," to remove plaques that remembered those who had "fallen for God and Spain"; and prohibited commemorative events at the Valley of the Fallen monument, where Franco is buried. The law also called for the one-sided monument to become a place of commemoration for all those killed in the Civil War. Little has been done to achieve the latter. The state also created funds to finance the exhumation of mass graves containing victims from both sides. (The PP government paid in 2002 for the exhumation and repatriation from Russia of the corpses of several Spanish volunteers from the División Azul sent by Franco to support Nazi troops during World War II.) The Association for the Recovery of Historical Memory, founded in 2000, has become very active in unearthing mass graves around Spain. The San Rafael cemetery in Malaga contains the remains of more than 4,400 people who were executed without trial between 1937 and 1951.

In 2008 Garzón declared the acts of repression committed by the Franco dictatorship to be crimes against humanity and began an investigation into cases of illegal detention and forced disappearances, involving the deaths of more than 114,000 people, committed between 1936 and 1951. This prompted a fringe far-right political group, Manos Limpias (Clean Hands), to bring legal action against Garzón on the grounds that he had knowingly overstepped his authority, in particular by contravening the 1977 amnesty law that covers crimes perpetrated during the Civil War and the dictatorship. (In 2008, the UN Human Rights Committee called on Spain to repeal the amnesty law and to ensure that its courts did not apply limitation periods to crimes against humanity.) Garzón was cleared of this charge in 2012, but was found to have overstepped the mark in another case brought against him for illegally ordering a wiretap in a corruption case. He was suspended for 11 years, thus ending his career in Spain.

Equally divisive was the entry on Franco in the dictionary of national biography published in 2011 by the Royal Academy of History, which described his regime as "authoritarian, but not totalitarian" and did not describe Franco as a dictator. The text, which provoked a row on a sectarian basis, was written by the octogenarian Professor Luis Suárez, a senior figure in the Brotherhood of the Valley of the Fallen, the mausoleum where Franco is buried. The emotions aroused in the cases of Garzón and the dictionary showed that the ghosts of the past have not been fully laid to rest.

What made the economy boom for so long?

The Socialists inherited from the previous Popular Party (PP) administration a fast-growing economy whose fundamentals—inflation, the budget deficit, and the level of public debt—were in good shape thanks to the PP's success in meeting the macroeconomic conditions for Spain to be a founder member of the euro zone as of 1999. Macroeconomic stability, coupled with some free-market reforms and the massive inflow of EU funds and foreign direct investment, locked Spain into a virtuous circle of sustained GDP growth. The engine of growth and massive job creation, however, was the unsustainable and labor-intensive construction sector, particularly the accelerated building of homes, which produced a lopsided economy. Between 1995 and 2007, eight million jobs were created. The labor force, which stood at 12 million in 1995 (the same size as two decades earlier), increased to more than 20 million in 2007. This period was known as one of *vacas gordas* (fat cows) and lamentably it was not used to introduce much-needed structural reforms. Investment in residential housing reached 9 percent of the GDP, a much higher proportion than in other parts of Europe. Housing starts during the Socialist period accelerated to 434,316 a year between 2004 and 2011, from an annual average of 269,391 under the PP between 1996 and 2003—far more than needed even in steady market conditions, which Spain's plainly were not. The country accounted for around 30 percent of all new homes built in the European Union between 2000 and 2009, although its economy only generated around 10 percent of the Union's total GDP.

There were several reasons for the construction boom. First, interest rates were very low after Spain adopted the euro in 1999. They fell from 14 percent (with the peseta) to 4 percent (with the euro) in a matter of weeks and continued to fall. In setting them, the European Central Bank was mainly guided by the economic environment in Germany and France, the largest economies. This one-size-fits-all monetary policy was not suited to Spain. As its inflation rate was higher, interest rates there were often close to zero in real terms. This encouraged borrowers to take out loans; mortgages were further stimulated by the tax breaks for buying a home. Spanish and foreign banks fell over themselves to provide finance and offered up to 110 percent loans for 40 years. German banks, in particular, funded those Spanish banks that needed extra financing for their loans. Second, property was viewed as a good investment in a country where home ownership was 85 percent (compared to a euro zone average of 60 percent) and a significant number of people had a second home (usually an apartment on the coast or a house in a village). House price rises averaged 12 percent a year during most of the 2000s and speculative investors made a killing before the collapse of the market. The *Economist* magazine said Spain's property prices were 44 percent overvalued in 2011.[3] Third, foreign demand for holiday and retirement homes. Fourth, the regionally based and unlisted *cajas de ahorros* (savings banks, similar to savings-and-loan institutions in the United States) were closely connected to politicians and businessmen in the areas where they operated, and property developers had vested interests in pushing property for all it was worth. Municipal authorities benefited from the reclassification of land for building purposes, as this increased their revenue (paltry from other sources), while building that took place on vacant land of a certain size entitled town halls to take possession of 10 percent of the land, which was then often sold back to the developer. This practice was fertile ground for corruption. Spaniards joked at the time that the easiest way to become a millionaire was to become a mayor. In 2006, at the peak of its economic boom, Spain accounted for one-quarter of the total number of 500 euro notes in circulation in the then 12 euro zone countries—much higher than what should correspond to the country's economic size. Ordinary Spaniards referred to these notes, used in large informal economy transactions, as "bin Ladens" (in reference to Osama bin Laden, the founder of al Qaeda), because everyone knew they existed and what they looked like but had never seen them. All in all, Spain's collective madness in the property sector was a tale of greed, cronyism, trafficking of influences, corruption, reckless lending, and a woeful lack of adequate supervision by the banking authorities. Newspapers during the boom period were stuffed with property and luxury car advertisements.

Spaniards and some Spanish companies borrowed heavily from the banks and went on a spending binge. Credit to the private sector at the height of the boom increased at an annual average of 23 percent between 2004 and 2007. Spain accounted at one stage for one quarter of the euro zone's total lending. Furthermore, the growth in credit was not balanced across the various sectors of the economy, but was concentrated in the real estate sector. Loans relating to real estate purchases, development, and construction in 2007 accounted for 62 percent of bank financing to the private sector. The gross debt of households and non-financial corporations doubled to a whopping 214 percent of the GDP between 2000 and 2010, when this same ratio stood at around 165 percent both in the euro zone as a whole and in the United States. This accumulation of debt by the private sector led to an increase in the Spanish net debit position vis-à-vis the rest of the world, which stood in 2011 at 92 percent of the GDP. This figure was close to that exhibited by Greece, Portugal, and Ireland, all of them around 100 percent and all of them bailed out by the European Union between 2010 and 2011. Countries such as France, Italy, the United Kingdom, and the United States showed net debit positions against the rest of the world of between 10 percent and 20 percent of their GDP. At the other extreme, Germany and the Netherlands had net asset positions in relation to the rest of the world of around 35 percent of their GDP.

The boom in the property sector would not have been possible without the influx of immigrant workers, mainly from non-EU countries, who themselves needed homes and, in turn, helped to sustain the housing boom. The number of non-EU immigrants reached 2.3 million in 2005 and their irregular situation (unlike EU immigrants, they have no automatic right to work in Spain) led the Socialist government to approve an amnesty that year. It benefited 578,000 people who were able to provide some form of employment contract and prove they had lived in Spain for at least six months. In 2006, the number of housing starts (762,214) was more than that of Germany, France, and Italy combined. Between 1998 and 2007, the stock of homes grew by 5.7 million (nearly 30 percent).

Spain created about one-third of new jobs in the European Union in 2006. The property sector, in particular, had a big knock-on impact on the rest of the economy. The Spanish economy expanded by a yearly average of just over 3 percent between 2004, when the Socialists took office, and 2008, when the economy took a nosedive, compared to 2.1 percent for the euro zone during that period. The unemployment rate had halved under the PP, from 22.8 percent in 1996 to 11.5 percent in early 2004 when the PP left office, and it continued to fall under the Socialists, to a low of 8 percent in 2007. Spain's per capita income rose from 91 percent of the average for the 27 European Union countries in 1996 to 101 percent in 2004 and a peak of 105 percent in 2007 (higher than Italy). The economic bonanza generated a surge in fiscal receipts and resulted in a budget surplus of 2.2 percent of the GDP in 2007 and a reduction in the level of public debt to 36.3 percent of the GDP. But it also produced a current account deficit in 2006 that, at $105 billion (8 percent of the GDP), was the second largest in the world in absolute terms after the much larger US economy. In 2007, the deficit was 10 percent of the GDP, underscoring the extent to which the economy had become overheated and uncompetitive, and Spaniards were living way beyond their means and on borrowed money.

What was the impact of the collapse of the property and construction sectors?

Spain's economic boom was built on shaky foundations, which began to crumble after the first signs of a global credit crunch in August 2007, following the subprime mortgage crisis in the United States, and particularly after September 2008 and the collapse of Lehman Brothers, which triggered the deepest downturn in the global economy since the Great Depression in the 1930s. Too much of the Spanish economy was built, literally, on bricks and cement and too little on knowledge. Spain's spending on R&D has traditionally been low (1.3 percent of the GDP in 2011, compared to a European Union average of 2.0 percent and more than 3.0 percent in the Nordic countries), and the country accounted in 2009 (latest available year) for only 0.5 percent of triadic patents (those filed at the European Patent Office, the United States Patent and Trademark Office, and the Japan Patent Office).

The construction and property sectors accounted for 18 percent of the GDP and 20 percent of employment at the height of the boom in 2006 and generated 30 percent of economic growth between 1997 and 2007. Such a lopsided economic model was not sustainable, and it was, to borrow the title of a novel by Gabriel García Márquez, a Chronicle of a Death Foretold. For more than a decade, the political class was happy to encourage phenomenal growth of this sector without giving thought to the bubble being created or what would happen after it burst. When it did burst in 2008, Spain's real economic growth plummeted from 3.6 percent in 2007 to 0.9 percent in 2008, and the country was plunged into recession between 2009 and 2013 (growth was anemic in 2011). Many banks and property developers went to the wall. The impact on government accounts was equally dramatic: rapidly falling revenues, and spending that continued to rise, as a large part of it was allotted for essential services such as health and education, turned a budget surplus of 1.9 percent of the GDP in 2007 into a deficit of 11.2 percent in 2009 (7 percent in 2012). Gross public debt jumped from 36.3 percent of the GDP in 2007, before the crisis, to 84 percent at the end of in 2012 and property sectors.

More than half of the over three million jobs shed between 2008 and 2012—to a total number of 5.9 million unemployed and an official jobless rate of 25 percent, the highest figure in the industrialized world—came from the construction and real estate sectors. The proportion of the working population unemployed for more than two years rose from 1.7 percent in 2007 to more than 10 percent in 2012 (double the EU rate). The youth unemployment rate (in the 16–24 age bracket), including those in education, reached 55 percent (excluding students and some other categories, the rate is still very high at around half that figure). Many of these unemployed people had left school at 16 and went to work in the construction sector. In 2007, at the height of the economic boom, 31 percent of those aged between 18 and 24 had left school at 16, double the average early school leavers rate for the European Union.[4] Some of these poorly qualified people returned to studying during the crisis, while those at school had no option but to stay on. In 2012, the early school leaving rate had declined to 25 percent.

The Organization for Economic Co-operation and Development (OECD) warned of the risk of a property bubble in 2004, four years before the bubble burst. The average price per square meter rose from €842 in 1996 to €1,888 in 2003, six times faster than the growth in wages. Jaime Caruana, the governor of the Bank of Spain, also called in 2004 for "an ordered adjustment through a slowdown in prices." The government, however, took no measures to cool down the property sector or the growth in bank lending fueling the boom. (In 1988 and 1989, at the time of another boom and before the launch of the euro, the Bank of Spain imposed a 10 percent annual growth limit on lending by banks.) Banks' outstanding loans to developers and construction companies rose from €33.5 billion in 2000 to €470 billion in 2008 (almost 50 percent of Spain's GDP). The stock of new and unsold homes rose from 195,184 in 2005 to 676,038 at the end of 2011. Including homes that were not completed after property developers went bust or abandoned their projects, and properties repossessed by banks, the number of unsold homes was estimated at more than one million, reportedly as many as in the United States, whose economy is six times larger than that of Spain.

A typical example of the property fiasco was the *Residencial Francisco Hernando* (named after the developer), 35 kilometers from Madrid, which was intended to triple the population of Seseña in the dry plains of Castile with 13,500 apartments. It would have been one of the biggest residential complexes in Spain. Once billed as the "Manhattan of La Mancha," only around 2,500 of the apartments had been sold when the property bubble burst in 2008.

As well as the housing debacle, regional governments poured money into infrastructure, much of which was not needed. One example is the new $1.1 billion airport at Ciudad Real, 160 kilometers from Madrid in the region of Castile La Mancha, which was run at the time by the Socialists (since 2011 by the Popular Party). Although private, it was backed by the regional government and partially funded by a local savings bank (controlled by the regional government) that went bust. The airport, with a runway capable of taking the A380 super-jumbos, was intended to relieve the pressure on Madrid's airport, as it is near the high-speed train network. Virtually its only traffic between December 2008 and 2011, when it closed, were private jets bringing wealthy visitors on hunting trips. This white elephant, an object of national ridicule, was aptly called Don Quixote, after the knight errant of Miguel de Cervantes's world-famous novel who finds it difficult to distinguish between reality and fiction. It was later renamed Ciudad Real Central Airport. In another example of reckless public spending, this time in the region of Valencia, controlled by the conservative Popular Party (PP), an airport was built at Castellón at a cost of more than $200 million and inaugurated in 2011 despite the failure of the regional government to secure a license to operate. An estimated $40 million was spent on advertising the airport. Visitors to the idle airport were greeted by a 24-meter-high statue dedicated to a local and controversial PP politician, crowned by an aluminum model aircraft. The politician, the head of the Castellón district council, was under judicial investigation in 2012 for corruption and tax evasion. Civic groups in the city of Valencia organized coach tours that followed the *ruta del despilfarro* (the route of squandering). Stops include the Formula 1 racing circuit, the City of Arts and Sciences (which includes a 4,000-seat opera house), a new football stadium, the enlarged parliament building, and, in stark contrast to this artificial opulence, a school with classrooms made from containers.

The profligate spending of regional governments, which accounted for 37 percent of total public expenditure, was a major factor behind Spain's ballooning budget deficit. It unnerved the markets in 2011 and 2012 and pushed up the risk premium on government bonds—the difference between Spain's 10-year bond yields and those of low-risk Germany—to more than 650 basis points, from an average of 8 basis points in 2007. At times the 10-year Spanish yield reached more than 700 basis points, a level that triggered the bailouts of Greece, Portugal, and Ireland in 2010 and 2011.

What happened to the rest of the economy?

The collapse of the property sector that triggered Spain's recession between 2009 and 2013, apart from a mild respite in 2011, left Spain even more heavily reliant on tourism, long a mainstay of the economy (around 12 percent of the GDP and 10 percent of the active labor force), and forced companies to export more. The tourism industry continued to flourish (more than such 57 million visitors a year, the fourth-largest such number in the world), partly thanks to the revolutions in the Arab world, which made tourists switch their holidays from these countries to Spain in 2011 and 2012. The Canary Islands off the coast of Africa, for example, received 12 million tourists in 2011, six times more than their combined population.

The recession made more Spanish companies sell abroad in order to survive, and some did so with remarkable success. Whereas before the introduction of the euro in 2002 Spain could devalue the peseta as a way to boost the competitiveness of its exports, since then it has only been able to increase competitiveness through productivity gains and squeezing profit margins. Exports of goods rose by $85 billion between 2009 and 2012, to $298 billion (21.5 percent of GDP). Exports covered 88 percent of imports, a record. The export surge and plummeting imports contributed to the sharp fall in Spain's current account deficit from 10 percent of the GDP in 2007 to less than 1 percent in 2012. Spain's per capita exports, however, were still relatively low at $5,339 (2010) compared to $7,458 for Italy and $15,474 for Germany.[5] The number of companies that exported in 2012, was a record 130,247, 12 percent more than in 2011. The country has an overall trade deficit, however, because of its persistently high bill for imported energy.

The export sector became more competitive after 2009. Spain's unit labor costs rose 38 percent between 1998 and 2009, compared to a 23 percent increase for the euro zone. During this period, wage deals continued to outstrip inflation, despite rising unemployment. Even in 2009, when the economy shrank by 3.7 percent, real wages rose by 3.2 percent. Wages have been falling in real terms since 2009, helping to make the economy more competitive. Nevertheless, Spain's position in the World Economic Forum's annual competitiveness ranking did not change (36th out of 144 countries in 2012, the same position as in 2011).

Traditionally an exporter of vegetables, fruit, and wine, Spain today exports a diversified range of products, including information and air traffic control systems, space navigation equipment, and cars (around 20 percent of total exports in a good year). While the United States, the United Kingdom, Germany, France, and Italy all lost global market share to varying degrees over the last decade, mainly to China and other emerging countries, Spain's share of world merchandise exports remained virtually unchanged at 1.7 percent, though it is considerably below that of Germany (8.3 percent), France (3.4 percent), and Italy (2.9 percent).

But for the exports drive, Spain's recession would have been deeper. The contribution of external demand to GDP growth was positive between 2008 and 2012 (the first time since 1997), but not sufficiently so as to offset the negative contribution of domestic demand and enable the economy to grow. Spain's external demand, unlike in Germany, an exporting power-house, has so far only been positive when the economy is in recession and companies have no option but to sell abroad.

The challenge for Spain was to overcome this structural problem and maintain the momentum of its exports when domestic demand picked up.

What austerity measures were taken?

José Luis Rodríguez Zapatero, the prime minister, refused to acknowledge the economy was in crisis for two years after the first signs of a meltdown appeared in 2008, and he won a second term in office. The Popular Party was also out of touch with reality. Its 2008 electoral program included a promise to create 2.2 million jobs, reduce the unemployment rate to 6.5 percent (the lowest level in post-Franco Spain), and accelerate GDP growth to 4 percent in 2012. In 2008, Zapatero was so confident about the strength of the economy that he introduced a $500 rebate for all taxpayers. The rebate was scrapped in 2009, when the economy was in recession for the first time since 1993, but few other cuts were made, which, coupled with plummeting tax revenues, caused the budget deficit to soar from 3.8 percent of the GDP in 2008 to an all-time high of 11.1 percent in 2009. The government's Keynesian countercyclical $11 billion Plan E, equivalent to the New Deal US President Franklin D. Roosevelt devised in response to the Great Depression, aimed to kick-start the economy in 2009 through public works. It had little effect. The 17-meter monument to Christopher Columbus was moved 100 meters back to the same spot in central Madrid where it had stood for almost 100 years. It was not until May 2010, by which time the European Union had agreed on a bailout of the Greek economy in the hope that this would stem the euro zone's existential crisis, that Zapatero stopped being in denial and engineered a U-turn in his economic policy.

As Spain is one of the 17 euro zone countries, devaluing the single currency was not a policy option, as it had been when the peseta existed, unless the country pulled out of the zone. The austerity drive included an average 5 percent cut in the salaries of 2.8 million civil servants (a freeze in 2011, continued in 2012 by the PP government), a $7.6 billion reduction in public-sector investment, a freeze on payments for five million pensioners, and the abolition of the $3,200 "baby check" for every newborn (introduced in 2007 to boost Spain's low birth rate). The country's per capita income dipped below the EU average in 2011 for the first time since 2001. It fell to 99 percent of the EU average in purchasing power standards from a peak of 105 percent in 2007.

Value-added tax was raised from 16 percent to 18 percent (to 21 percent in September 2012) and labor market reforms, at a time when unemployment was over 20 percent and rising, were imposed by decree as employers and trade unions failed to reach agreement on a package of measures after nearly two years of talks. Severance payments for workers on permanent contracts dismissed for fair reasons were lowered from 45 days to 33 days of salary for each year worked. According to the World Bank, redundancy costs in Spain, before the reform, averaged 56 weeks of wages, twice the OECD level. The public pension system was also reformed; and the retirement age gradually increased from 65 to 67 (fully in force as of 2027), and the number of years of contributions to qualify for the maximum pension raised from 35 to 37. Lastly, in a rare display of putting aside their differences, the Socialists and the Popular Party wrote a German-style "golden rule" deficit cap into the constitution, the first big change since the document was drafted in 1978. Under the reform, Spain must stick to a long-term deficit cap except in times of natural disaster, recession, or extraordinary emergencies. The limit for the structural deficit (the portion of a country's budget deficit that is not the result of changes in the economic cycle) was set at 0.4 percent of the annual GDP from 2020.

What caused the banking crisis?

Spanish banks were not exposed to the US subprime mortgage crisis, but they were heavily exposed to toxic real estate assets following the collapse of the country's property market in 2008. The government, however, apparently did not realize this. Prime Minister José Luis Rodríguez Zapatero told a meeting of Wall Street bankers in New York, nine days after the collapse of Lehman Brothers in September 2008, that "Spain has perhaps the most solid financial system in the world. It has a standard of regulation and supervision recognized internationally for its quality and rigor." After the bubble burst and Spain went into recession, the loan defaults of property developers and construction firms as a percentage of total bank lending to these two sectors (known as the non-performing loan, or NPL, ratio) surged from a mere 0.6 percent in 2007 to more than 25 percent in 2012. The total amount of non-performing loans of Spain's banks represented 10.3 percent of lending to all sectors in 2012 (excluding the toxic loans placed in a specially created "bad bank"), up from 0.7 percent in 2006.

The banking crisis was concentrated in the regionally based savings banks, known as *cajas*, which accounted for around half the domestic banking system. They were particularly hard hit by loan defaults, and this sparked a banking collapse similar in depth to that of the savings-and-loans crisis in the United States in the late 1980s. The *cajas* date from the 19th century and were created to help the "less fortunate classes." Based to some extent on the German model, they are not limited companies and so do not have share capital. They channel funds into community projects instead of paying dividends. They are governed by a general assembly and boards of directors packed with political appointees, local businessmen, and savers. Over the years the large *cajas*, such as Caja Madrid and the Barcelona-based La Caixa, moved on from their humble origins as regionally based quasi-charitable institutions to become financial services groups on a par with commercial banks. They also took stakes in companies. The removal of restrictions in 1989 on establishing branches outside their home regions enabled the *cajas* to expand around Spain, and they did so at an inexorable pace. The number of savings bank branches rose from 13,642 in 1990 to a peak of 25,001 in September 2008, while the number of branches of the much more prudent commercial banks, most notably the two big ones, Santander and BBVA, dropped over the same period from 16,917 to 15,657.

The first to fall was Caja Castilla La Mancha (CCM) in March 2009, when the Bank of Spain (the country's central bank) took over its administration. Among other reckless projects, CCM had provided finance to the building of the white elephant airport at Ciudad Real. Its seizure was the first bank rescue in Spain in 16 years. Two other *cajas*, CajaSur, mainly controlled by the Catholic Church, and Caja de Ahorros del Mediterraneo (CAM), based in Valencia, ground zero of the property collapse, were also seized.

In a decade, the standing and reputation of the Spanish banking system moved from that of an internationally hailed model to one of disgrace. The Bank of Spain had pioneered in 2000 an innovative countercyclical provisioning policy that created a cushion during the upward phases of the economic cycle in order to soften the impact of bad loans on banks' earnings during periods of lower growth, when defaults are higher. The listed commercial banks, particularly Santander and BBVA, the two biggest, which between them account for around one-third of Spain's banking system, used this macroprudential policy tool to build up a buffer of provisions that enabled them to withstand the crisis relatively well. But supervision of the savings banks was woefully inadequate and the quality of governance left a lot to be desired. An internal report by inspectors at the Bank of Spain (the central bank), leaked in 2012, claimed the bank's management "looked the other way" when staff found indications of wrongdoing in the banks they were supervising.

"In the real estate and financial bubble years there was a sort of euphoria which led to the risks that were accumulating to not be seen, or not wish to be seen," said Luis Linde, the governor of the Bank of Spain (central bank), who took over from Miguel Ángel Fernández Ordóñez in June 2012.[6] Ordóñez quit a month before the end of his term in office as a result of government criticism of his handling of the banking crisis. "It was as if nobody wanted to forecast scenarios of recession, interest-rate rises or collapses in funding," said Linde. As George Orwell, the British writer, observed in 1946, "to see what is in front of one's nose needs a constant struggle."[7] Spain's political and financial elite failed to do so.

What steps were taken to resolve the financial crisis?

In 2009, against the backdrop of a banking crisis in many other EU countries, the government set up the Fund for the Orderly Restructuring of the Banking System (FROB) to promote with public aid a series of mergers and integrations between savings banks. The number of savings banks declined from 46 to 11 between 2009 and 2012, mainly due to mergers forced through by the Bank of Spain (the central bank). The FROB took stakes in some of the banks. In January 2011, seven ailing savings banks—including Caja Madrid, the second biggest controlled by the Popular Party (PP)—merged to form Bankia, the fourth-largest lender, which was floated on the Madrid Stock Exchange in July of that year on the basis of unaudited accounts. Bankia and its parent, Banco Financiero y Ahorros, were touted as the largest bank in Spain in terms of domestic business, with $455 billion in loans and deposits and a 10 percent market share. Officials hoped the consolidation of these institutions into one large bank would resolve the savings bank crisis, but instead the botched merger created the biggest banking catastrophe in Spain's history. In May 2012, the PP government, which had ousted the Socialists and returned to power in December 2011 (see chapter 7), nationalized Bankia, headed by Rodrigo Rato, a former PP economy minister and managing director of the International Monetary Fund, after Deloitte refused to sign the 2011 accounts. Two months before the nationalization, the Bank of Spain accused Bankia in an internal report of "not reflecting in its accounts the real bad debts of its lending portfolio."[8] A report presented to Bankia's board by one of its directors in December 2011 said the bank had 280 real estate developer clients (borrowers) who were mostly insolvent.[9]

José Ignacio Goirigolzarri, a former chief executive of the big commercial bank BBVA, was brought out of retirement to replace Rato and requested $25 billion in new emergency capital, on top of earlier state aid of $6 billion. Bankia restated its 2011 results to reflect a net loss of $4 billion instead of the reported net profit of $413 million. The bank made a loss of $25.2 billion in 2012, the biggest ever in Spain's corporate history. In return for receiving $23.5 billion of EU rescue funds in 2012, which took its total amount of state aid to $47 billion, Bankia has to cut around 6,000 jobs (28 percent of its staff) and close to 40 percent of its branches by 2015.

The more than 350,000 retail investors who bought preferred stock in Bankia in the belief they were a safe investment saw their savings virtually wiped out by a share price that dropped 80 percent in the bank's first year.

Tougher measures were adopted regarding accounting for provisions, tightening the treatment of foreclosed property and land and of real estate collateral, and shortening the provisioning schedule for doubtful loans. Capital requirements were also increased and a new minimum core capital ratio set at 8 percent (10 percent for banks highly dependent on wholesale funding markets). Stress tests were conducted on nearly all banks in 2010, 2011, and 2012 in an exercise overseen by the European Banking Authority to gauge the extent to which the banks would survive various recession scenarios. The Socialist government announced in July 2011 that these tests "clearly demonstrated the Spanish financial system to be of a sound and solvent nature." The quality of the first tests, however, proved to be inadequate, as practically nobody had foreseen that Spain would still be in recession in 2012 and 2013. They were also undermined by the intensified deterioration of the euro zone crisis. The PP government, which took office in

December 2011, requested an independent assessment of the degree of solvency of the banking system by two international consulting firms. These results showed in September 2012 that the banking system as a whole would need $78 billion in capital in a worst-case scenario to maintain a capital ratio of 6 percent. This figure was lower than the EU bailout of up to $125 billion, agreed upon before this stress test for those banks in need of recapitalization in return for setting up a "bad bank" for toxic property assets, reforming the woefully inadequate supervisory system, which had failed to spot the crisis, and regular updates on the ailing banks to the European Commission, the European Central Bank, and the International Monetary Fund. Other measures required extra provisions for real estate loans and more core capital. Overall, the provisions for bad loans made by banks between 2007 and 2012 exceeded $250 billion, equivalent to more than 20 percent of the Spanish GDP in 2011. The average coverage of loans to the real estate sector increased from 18 percent at the end of 2011 to 45 percent a year later.

The two largest banks, Santander, the euro zone's largest bank by market capitalization, and BBVA, had no extra capital needs, as the stress tests showed they were very solvent even in the most adverse scenarios. The Financial Stability Board included both these banks in November 2012 in its updated list of the world's 29 most systemically important banks and in the lowest risk category. These banks are considered too big to fail.

What was the indignant movement?

The Spanish public expressed outrage against the rate of unemployment (the highest in a developed country), austerity measures, the collapse of savings banks, and the millionaire salaries and severance payments of senior executives. This outrage came to a head on May 15, 2011, when tens of thousands of disenchanted young people occupied the Puerta del Sol square in Madrid, the heart of the city, and set up camp for a month. The grassroots movement, known as 15-M and articulated through mobile phones and the Internet, quickly gathered supporters around Spain and inspired the Occupy Wall Street movement. Supporters ranged from anti-capitalists, workers who had lost their jobs, and pensioners hit by cuts to their payments, to homeowners whose properties had been repossessed because they could not pay the mortgage and university students who, with youth unemployment approaching 50 percent (for under-25-year-olds), saw no future.

The movement of *los indignados* (the indignant movement) had no particular ideology and caught the political class by surprise. Its supporters were united by their anger at the two main political parties, the Socialists and the Popular Party (PP), because they spent more time squabbling than seeking a common path to overcome Spain's economic crisis. Opinion polls regularly showed politicians as the least respected group and part of Spain's problems instead of the channel to solve them.

The 15-M movement turned its back on traditional top-down political parties and trade unions and, in a bottom-up approach, targeted specific issues such as banking and reforming the electoral laws, which favor the large parties. Up to 80 percent of Spaniards said they supported the protesters. An unlikely hero of the movement was Michael Banks, a child actor in the 1964 Disney musical *Mary Poppins*. His face was featured on posters pinned to the walls of the Puerta del Sol square, as he had demanded his money back from the Dawes Tomes Mousley Grubbs Fidelity Fiduciary Bank and started a run. A nationwide network was created to draw attention to the plight of people who had lost their jobs and, unable to meet their mortgage repayments, faced the foreclosure of their homes, as well as a legal requirement to repay the loans used to buy them. Mortgage law in Spain is among the toughest in Europe. Homeowners remain liable for what they owe on their mortgage loan even after returning the house to the bank, if the sale of the property does not cancel out the entire debt. Around 350,000 properties (residential and land) were repossessed between

2008 and 2012. In some cases, people blocked streets and prevented homeowners from being evicted. (The PP responded to mounting social pressure and several suicides over home evictions by issuing a decree in November 2012, a year after it took office, which suspended them for two years for the most needy. A ruling by the European Court of Justice in March 2013 forced the PP government to change the mortgage law and tighten foreclosures.

While the PP sought to portray the 15-M supporters as anarchists (they were in fact very well behaved and bouts of street violence were very rare), the Socialists and in particular the communist-led United Left hoped to channel the dissent to their advantage.

What made the political class so unpopular?

Spain's politicians were perceived as part of the country's deep problems, instead of the vehicle with which to solve them. Opinion polls showed the political class at the national, regional, and municipal levels as the country's third most serious problem (as determined by one in every four respondents) after unemployment and other economic issues. Political parties were the least approved of 34 institutions and social groups. Doctors headed the approval ranking. Discontent with the political class, particularly with the two main parties, the Socialists and the conservative Popular Party, was due to a spate of scandals involving embezzlement of public funds, constant bickering among the political elite and its failure to put aside partisan differences and interests and agree to measures for the good of the country, the politicization of state institutions, the snail's pace at which the judiciary system moves (its bureaucracy and procedures are mainly paper-based and have hardly changed since the 19th century), and a lack of an effective system of checks and balances and of democracy within political parties. Spaniards elect their politicians from "closed" voting lists drawn up by the party leadership. Disloyal party members can be punished by placing them so low on the list that they stand little chance of entering parliament. The political class is regarded as an extractive elite.[10] According to some estimates, up to 300,000 jobs in Spain are political appointments.

Such was the disillusionment with politicians that on the eve of the November 2011 general election, 75 percent of voters said they had little or no confidence in the Socialist candidate, Alfredo Pérez Rubalcaba, and 66 percent said the same for the PP's candidate Mariano Rajoy, who won. Spain was not unique in having a discredited political class, but the depth of feelings against it was extraordinarily intense and led to demonstrations outside parliament in Madrid in 2012 and 2013 with banners that read *Que se vayan todos* ("Away with all of them"). A judge in 2012, Santiago Pedraz, enraged the political elite when he rejected the case against the organizers of the protests brought by the police, saying it was justified by the "generally recognized decadence of the political class."

Did the center-periphery tension improve under Zapatero?

Broadly speaking, relations between the central government and nationalists in the Basque Country remained fraught during the eight years of Socialist rule, while those with Catalonia became more problematic. The Basque parliament approved in December 2004 the plan of Juan José Ibarretxe, the *lehendakari* (head) of the Basque government, for a "free association" of the Basque Country with Spain, including the right to self-determination. It was inspired by the status of Puerto Rico with the United States, and was aimed at unilaterally changing the Basque statute of autonomy. The plan, which would have involved a referendum, was rejected by the Spanish parliament in February 2005 (by 319 votes against 29 in favor).

The Basque separatist group ETA (Euskadi Ta Askatasuna—Basque Homeland and Freedom) announced a cease-fire in March 2006, which was broken at the end of that year when the group planted a bomb in a car park at Madrid's airport and killed two Ecuadorean immigrants. The government had invested considerable political capital that year in trying to solve the conflict. This attack ended any hope that the ETA would disband voluntarily while arguing it had not been defeated by the Spanish state. It marked a turning point and led the Socialists (and the Popular Party after it returned to office at the end of 2011) to implement a policy toward the group based solely on "law and order" and not negotiations, which all previous prime ministers had attempted. The Socialists teamed up with the PP after winning, between them, a majority of the seats in the 2009 Basque parliamentary elections and dislodged the Basque Nationalist Party from power, as it did not gain sufficient votes to continue governing.

The central government was understandably wary of the ETA's "definitive" cease-fire on October 20, 2011, to end 43 years of terrorism to establish a sovereign Basque state. The group, which has a long history of broken promises and failed truces, did not disarm and reach a Good Friday–style agreement of the sort reached in Northern Ireland in 1998 between the British government and the Irish Republican Army (IRA). The cease-fire came at a time when the ETA was considerably weakened by the arrest of activists, particularly in France, the seizure of caches of arms, and the dismantling of its illegal sources of financing. There was also growing pressure from part of the *izquierda abertzale* (patriotic left) and from several hundred ETA prisoners that the cause of independence would be best served by participating in mainstream politics. A coalition of the ETA's political allies called Bildu had won 26 percent of Basque votes in municipal elections in May 2011 (six months before the ETA's cease-fire), the second-largest share of the vote after the center-right Basque Nationalist Party. These results led the ETA to recognize that the solution to the Basque conflict would come "through a democratic process that takes the will of the Basque people as its maximum point of reference, and dialogue and negotiation as its tools." The language of this statement was very similar to the declaration made three days before by an international peace conference in San Sebastián. Among the participants was former UN Secretary General Kofi Anan, and the group called for an end to violence and a political resolution of the Basque conflict. One month after the cease-fire, Amaiur, another Basque coalition in favor of independence, did well in the November 2011 general election and entered the national parliament in Madrid for the first time with seven seats, two more than the Basque Nationalist Party, traditionally the most-voted-for party in the Basque Country.

In Catalonia, which accounts for around one-fifth of the Spanish economy and 16 percent of the population, the regional parliament's vote in 2005 in favor of greater autonomy led all parties in the national parliament in Madrid except for the Popular Party (PP) to agree to consider the proposal for a new statute. The PP feared a new statute would lead to the breakup of Spain as a unified state. A new home rule charter granting greater control over areas such as infrastructure, work permits for immigrants in the region, the judiciary, taxes, and negotiating rights with the European Union on matters affecting Catalonia was approved in 2006 by the regional and national parliaments and ratified by Catalans in a referendum. Three-quarters of Catalan voters approved the new self-government charter, against 21 percent who rejected it. The abstention rate, however, was high at 51 percent. The PP referred the charter to the Constitutional Court. In June 2010, the court upheld all but 14 of the charter's 233 articles but stopped short of approving some of the most controversial points, including the recognition of Catalan as the "preferred language." It did, however, accept the most contentious point of the statute's preamble, which defined Catalonia as a "nation," saying it was a historical and cultural term and had "no legal value" that would violate Spain's constitution.

Most of the Catalan political class protested, including the Catalan Socialist Party, which headed the three-way coalition government in the region at the time (defeated by the conservative nationalist coalition Convergence and Union, CiU, in

the November 2010 election, though it did not win an absolute majority). Ernest Benach, the president of the Catalan parliament, claimed the court's ruling opened a "crisis of state"
because it "ignores the will of Catalan citizens." The court's
verdict marked a turning point for Catalan nationalists, as it
convinced many of them, including Jordi Pujol, CiU president
of the region's government from 1980 to 2003 and the preeminent nationalist leader during the transition to democracy, that
Catalonia no longer belonged inside Spain.

Who is Mariano Rajoy?

Mariano Rajoy became leader of the conservative Partido
Popular (Popular Party, PP) in 2004 when José María Aznar
decided not to run for a third term in office. Rajoy had been
minister of public administrations (1996–1999), minister of
education and culture (1999–2000), deputy prime minister
and interior minister (2001–2002), and deputy prime minister and minister of the presidency (2002–2003) in the two PP
governments. The PP lost the general election in 2004 and in
2008, but Rajoy remained as the PP leader. He became prime
minister in December 2011 after his party swept the Socialists
out of power.

He was born in 1955 in Santiago de Compostela, the capital
of Galicia, the region in the northwest of Spain from where
other conservative political leaders have hailed, including
General Franco and Manuel Fraga. His paternal grandfather
was one of the architects of the statute of autonomy of Galicia
during the Second Republic (1931–1939), which was not implemented because of the Civil War, and his father was a jurist
and president of the provincial court of Pontevedra. At the age
of 23, Rajoy passed the tough competitive exam to enter the
civil service and became Spain's youngest-ever property regis-
trar, a lucrative and safe job.

He entered politics in 1981 when he was elected to the
inaugural legislature of the Galician parliament as a member

of the right-wing Alianza Popular (Popular Alliance, AP), the precursor of the PP (established in 1989). By then Spain had a quasi-federal system. The PP is the dominant political force in Galicia. Rajoy was the director general of institutional relations in the region's first *Xunta* (government) and deputy president (1986–1987). He was elected to the national parliament in Madrid in 1986 as head of the AP's list for Pontevedra and has been an MP since then.

Rajoy implemented in 2012 and 2013 the severest austerity measures in Spain's post-Franco democracy. In 2013, he was caught up in a slush fund scandal after pages of a ledger allegedly handwritten by Luis Bárcenas, the PP's former treasurer and senator, were published in *El País*, the leading daily, and showed secret cash payments to PP leaders, including Rajoy, and donations to the party from companies over 18 years. Bárcenas said the handwriting was not his, and Rajoy denied receiving any payments. Rajoy also responded by publishing his tax returns, but this did not dispel the allegations. In separate cases, Bárcenas was under investigation after a judge discovered $29 million in Swiss bank accounts held by him, and a circle of businessmen and PP politicians was accused of bribery, money laundering, and tax evasion in a case known as Gürtel.

7

WHAT LIES AHEAD?

The conservative Popular Party (PP) of Mariano Rajoy trounced the Socialists in the November 2011 general election and scored its best-ever result (see table 7.1). The PP increased its number of seats in parliament from 154 to 186, giving it an absolute majority with 44.6 percent of the vote, while the Socialists under Alfredo Pérez Rubalcaba, a former interior minister and party spokesman, dropped from 169 to 110 seats and saw their share of the vote plummet from 43.6 percent to 28.7 percent. José Luis Rodríguez Zapatero, the incumbent prime minister, did not run for a third term. The discredited Socialists lost more than 4 million votes, but the PP gained fewer than 600,000. Voters deserted the Socialists mainly for the hard-line United Left, which increased its number of seats from two to 11, and the centrist Progress and Democracy Union (from one to five), or abstained. The next election is not due until the end of 2015.

Spain, the euro zone's fourth-largest economy, was mired in uncharted territory. The PP had to tackle a crisis on five fronts: economic (collapse of an unsustainable economic model excessively based on the labor-intensive construction sector), financial (high budget deficit and public debt burden), institutional (a major loss of confidence in the political elite), social (more than 1.7 million households with no members working), and constitutional (the push in Catalonia for independence).

Table 7.1 Results of General Elections, 1977–2011 (% of total votes)

	1977	1979	1982	1986	1989	1993	1996	2000	2004	2008	2011
UCD (centrist)	34.5	35.0	–	–	–	–	–	–	–	–	–
Socialists	29.4	30.5	48.3	44.1	39.6	38.8	37.6	34.7	42.6	43.6	28.7
Communists[1]	9.4	10.8	4.0	4.6	9.1	9.6	10.5	5.5	4.9	3.8	5.4
Conservatives[2]	8.2	6.0	26.5	26.0	25.8	34.8	38.8	45.2	37.6	40.1	44.6
Catalan[3]	2.8	2.7	3.7	5.0	5.0	4.9	4.6	4.2	3.2	3.0	4.1
Basque[4]	1.6	1.5	1.9	1.5	1.2	1.2	1.3	1.5	1.6	1.2	1.3
Other	14.1	13.5	15.6	18.8	19.3	10.7	7.2	8.9	10.1	8.3	15.9

(1) Spanish Communist Party, known as United Left as of the 1986 election. (2) Popular Alliance, known as the Popular Party as of the 1989 election. (3) Center-right Democratic Agreement for Catalonia, known as Convergence and Union as of the 1979 election. (4) Center-right Basque Nationalist Party.

UCD = Union of the Democratic Center.

Source: Interior Ministry.

Spain's gross government debt to GDP ratio more than doubled between 2007 and 2012 to 84 percent, and the budget deficit in 2012 was still very high at 7 percent of the GDP (10 percent, including the euro zone bailout funds for the country's ailing banks). The government committed itself to lowering the deficit to below the EU threshold of 3 percent in 2014, which is a Herculean and probably impossible task. Rajoy hoped to avoid following in the footsteps of Cyprus, Greece, Ireland, and Portugal and having to seek a full sovereign bailout from the EU.

The most critical problem is to get the economy moving again and create jobs in a country with a seasonally adjusted unemployment rate of 26 percent in 2013. Spain is not expected to come out of its five-year recession (growth in 2011 was anemic) until 2014, and even then expansion will be weak. The economy needs to grow by more than 2 percent in real terms in order to create jobs in net terms. It will take years for the property sector to return to even normal size. The economic model can only become more sustainable if it is more knowledge-based and export-focused.

The depth of Spain's crisis is such that the country, with 11 percent of the euro zone's GDP and a population of 47 million, accounted at the end of 2012 for 31 percent of the zone's 18.7 million total jobless (5.9 million), whereas Germany (population 82 million and 30 percent of the GDP) accounted for only 15 percent of the unemployed (2.9 million). Spain's jobless rate was the country's highest ever and close to five times Germany's rate of 5.3 percent, the lowest since reunification in 1991, and it was forecast to remain at around 25 percent until 2015. This disproportionate difference cannot be explained away by Germany's *kurzabeit* system, under which companies agree to avoid laying off workers and instead reduce their working hours, with the government making up some of the employees' lost income, or by Spain's still too rigid labor market. Its hiring and firing system was ranked 129th out of 144 countries in the World Economic Forum's 2012 competitiveness league. The problem was as much related to Spain's lopsided economic model, which created hundreds of thousands of jobs when the economy was booming and destroyed them equally massively during the recession. Spain has the developed world's highest Okun coefficient (i.e., the greatest sensitivity of employment to changes in the GDP).

Spain's youth unemployment for those aged 16 to 24 was even more dramatic in 2013, at 55 percent. This staggering figure, based on the methodology employed by all EU countries to calculate youth unemployment, is often misunderstood to mean that half of young people are jobless, as opposed to being in education or not seeking work, which is not the case. The "real" unemployment rate for this age bracket was still high, at more than 22 percent. More worrying still was that more than one quarter of those aged between 15 and 29 were not in employment, education, or training (known as NEETs), a figure around 10 points above the OECD's average. These people form a "lost generation," as not only are they unemployed but many are also poorly qualified. Experience shows that if a young person is not on the job ladder by 24 they are likely to suffer the consequences for the rest of their lives. The gap between rich and poor, as measured by the Gini coefficient, reached its highest level in 2011 since records were kept. The coefficient, where zero is perfect equality and 100 absolute inequality, was 34, the second highest in the EU after Latvia.[1]

The economic model shows itself incapable of creating jobs on a sustained basis. Given the state of the education system and the large pool of unskilled workers, it will be very difficult to change the model. One in every four people in Spain between the ages of 18 and 24 were early school leavers in 2012, double the EU average but down from a peak of one-third during the economic boom, when students dropped out of school and flocked in droves to work in the construction sector.[2] Results in the OECD's Pisa tests in reading, mathematics, and scientific knowledge for 15-year-old students and for fourth-grade children in the TIMS and PIRLS tests are poor;

no Spanish university is among the world's top 200 in the main academic rankings (up to 35 percent of students drop out before graduation and only a third complete their studies on time); and research and development and innovation spending, at 1.3 percent of the GDP, is way below that of other developed economies.

In these conditions, a much more knowledge-based economy is a pipe dream, compounded by the PP government's cuts in R&D and education spending, as part of its austerity measures to get to grips with the budget deficit and public debt. Furthermore, the decision taken in 2013 by the US company Las Vegas Sands, headed by the billionaire Sheldon Adelson, to site Europe's largest casino, conference, and hotels complex on the outskirts of Madrid, which will create tens of thousands of jobs, accentuates the already skewed economic model.

There is a rising tide of frustration, most visibly seen in the movement of the indignant and reflected in opinion polls. It has been kept at bay by Spain's still-strong extended-family network, which looks after its own during times of crisis, although this family network is beginning to weaken under the magnitude of unemployment. Grandparents with pensions were increasingly supporting households, particularly those where all of its members were unemployed. On top of this, the unofficial economy is estimated to represent around a fifth of Spain's GDP and offers a cushion to workers during economic crises.

The crisis has raised questions about the sustainability of Spain's welfare state, virtually built from scratch in the last 40 years, and of its quasi-federal system of 17 autonomous regions, introduced after the 1978 democratic constitution. Spending on both could have been sustained as long as tax receipts kept on growing, which they did until the decade-long economic boom petered out in 2008.

As regards the quasi-federal system, the alternatives facing Spain are to recentralize the state, the option favored by the PP, or to move toward a German-style cooperative federalism under which regional governments would have to be more fiscally responsible and not, as in the past, happy to spend and go to the central government with a begging bowl in times of crisis instead of using their (limited) powers to raise revenues for fear of losing voter support. In Catalonia, the richest region, the crisis has fueled nationalists' push for independence via an illegal referendum on the issue. The confrontation between the center and Catalonia has threatened to unravel the constitutional settlement that so successfully enabled Spain to move from the Franco dictatorship to democracy and fragment the country.

Artur Mas, the premier of Catalonia and the leader of the center-right Convergence and Union (CiU) Party, called a snap election in November 2012 in a bid to win an absolute majority and have a free hand to push for a referendum on independence. The election followed a massive rally in favor of independence, attended by an estimated 1.5 million people two months earlier, and after Mas failed to win agreement from Rajoy for greater fiscal autonomy. Catalan nationalists were aggrieved at transferring what they regard as a disproportionate share of their wealth to Madrid for distribution to the poorer regions. They blame the central government for the severe spending cuts in their region. The CiU, however, won only 50 of the 135 seats in the Catalan parliament, down from 62 in 2010. The more radical and older Catalan Republican Left (ERC), a separatist party, more than doubled the number of its seats to 21, while the Socialists (in favor of a more federal state) dropped from 28 to 20 seats for its worst result ever in Catalonia. The PP (in favor of keeping the present arrangement) won 19 seats, one more. Overall, parties in favor of a referendum on independence gained 87 of the Catalan parliament's 135 seats, making a referendum possible. Voter turnout was close to 70 percent, the highest for a Catalan regional election in nearly 30 years.

The Spanish constitution gives the central government "exclusive competence" on the authorization of referendums,

Table 7.2 Basic Socioeconomic Statistics, 1975–2012

	1975[1]	2012[1]
Population (million)	36.0	47.2[2]
Foreign population	165,000	5.7 million[2]
Foreign population (% of total)	0.4	12.1[2]
Unemployment rate (%)	4.7	26.2
Nominal GDP ($million)	111,442	1,387,589
Per capita GDP ($)	3,186	29,360[3]
GDP structure (% of total)		
Agriculture	9.0	2.7
Industry	39.0	26.0
Services	52.0	71.3
Employment by sectors (% of total jobs)		
Agriculture	21.8	4.4
Industry and construction	37.8	20.7
Services	40.4	74.9
Exports of goods and services (% of GDP)	10.4	32.1
Imports of goods and services (% of GDP)	11.9	31.1
Number of tourists (million)	27.3	57.7
Consumer price inflation (%)	17.2 (av. ann. incr. 1972–77)	3.0

(Continued)

Table 7.2 (Continued)

	1975[1]	2012[1]
Gross national saving (% of GDP)	25.5	18.8 (2011)
Public debt (% of GDP)	42.3 (1985)	84.0
Public spending (% of GDP)	30.4 (average 1974–85)	43.6 (2011)
Total receipts from taxes and social security contributions (% of GDP)	18.4	32.4 (2011)
Inward stock of foreign direct investment ($billion)	5.1 (1980)	634.5 (2011)
Outward stock of Spanish investment ($billion)	1.9 (1980)	640.3 (2011)
Spending on R&D (% of GDP)	0.35	1.3 (2011)
Passenger cars per 1,000 population	123	478 (2009)
Average number of children per woman	2.8	1.3
Proportion of births outside marriage (%)	1.4 (1970)	32 (2009)
UN human development index[4]	0.680 (1980)	0.885
Average life expectancy at birth (years)	73.3	81.6
Percentage of population under the age of 15	27.8 (1970)	15.3[5]
Percentage of population over the age of 65	9.7 (1970)	17.7[5]
Early abandonment of education (%)[6]	17.7	24.9

(1) Unless otherwise stated and year-end. (2) January 1, 2012. (3) GDP at the end of 2012 divided by the population at the beginning of that year. (4) The maximum value is one. The index is based on life expectancy at birth, mean years of schooling, expected years of schooling, and per capita income. (5) October 2012. (6) The percentage of people aged 18–24 who have only lower secondary education or less and are no longer in education or training.

Source: Eurostat, National Statistics Office of Spain (INE), UN Human Development Reports, World Bank, and the United Nations Conference on Trade and Development (UNCTAD).

Table 7.3 Spain Today: Some Economic and Socioeconomic Realities*

Global Ranking	Description
Top 5	Longest years of healthy life (out of 18 European countries and the US)
Top 5	Largest installed capacity of solar energy
Top 5	Largest international manager of infrastructure
Top 5	Biggest producer of olive oil
Top 5	Biggest producer of sparkling wine (*cava*)
Top 5	2nd largest high-speed rail network after China
Top 5	2nd largest number of sites (44) in UNESCO's World Heritage List
Top 5	4th largest tourist destination in terms of visitors
Top 10	9th largest stock of inward foreign direct investment
Top 10	9th largest stock of outward direct investment
Top 10	9th longest life expectancy at birth
Top 15	11th in the Elcano Global Presence Index (out of 55 countries)
Top 15	12th largest producer of vehicles (2012; in 2011 it was 9th)
Top 15	13th largest economy in purchasing power parity terms
Top 25	23rd in the United Nations' Human Development Index (out of 187 countries)
Top 25	25th in the Democracy Index of the Economist Intelligence Unit, ahead of France
Top 30	30th in Transparency International's ranking of perceived levels of public sector corruption (out of 176 countries)

(*) The figures were the latest available at the end of 2012.

Source: The Lancet, IMF, Economist Intelligence Unit, UN Human Development Report 2013, World Investment Report 2011 (UNCTAD), ANFAC, the World Tourism Organization, Transparency International, Elcano Royal Institute, and the Spanish Foreign Ministry.

and Madrid has already ruled one out for Catalonia. The only legal way to trigger a process that results in the independence of any region was through a constitutional amendment, which would require a large majority in the Spanish parliament, new elections, and approval in a referendum held throughout the country. The Catalan government's determination to hold a referendum by the end of 2014 set it on a collision course with the central government in Madrid and if successfully held would also put wind in the sails of the independence movement in the Basque Country, where the pro-independence Bildu became the second-largest party in the Basque parliament in that region's elections in October 2012, scoring its best-ever result.

Lastly, a clean broom needs to be swept through the discredited political class, and some of the state's institutions colonized by the political class with a consequent loss of independence, particularly the *Consejo General del Poder Judicial* (General Council of the Judiciary), the body that oversees the judicial system, and the Constitutional Court. Opinion polls regularly show that Spaniards have a very low view of their politicians and of parliament. This is a worrying development in a democracy that has existed for less than 40 years. The country has one of the least open governments in the developed world. Compared to other countries in which citizens can regularly consult public contracts, spending, lawsuits and government reports via the Internet, the Spanish government has been extremely cautious over allowing citizens to access even basic information. As a result of popular pressure, this situation looks finally to be changing in 2013.

Spain has been through tough times before and will emerge successfully if it pulls together, as it did during the transition to democracy, a marvelous collective effort. The country has made tremendous strides since then (see tables 7.1 and 7.2). Another effort will be required to put the country back on a sustainable path.

NOTES

Introduction

1. Portugal's Antonio de Oliveria Salazar came in a close second.
2. Cited in "El valor de la marca España," by José Luis Barbería (*El País*, June 19, 2006). José María Aznar met George W. Bush in Crawford, Texas, in February 2003.

Chapter 1

1. Julián Marías, *Understanding Spain* (Michigan: University of Michigan Press, 1992), 205–233. The term became more widely known after Julián Juderías published a book on the subject in 1914 (*La Leyenda Negra*, Madrid: La Ilustración Española y Americana). He called the legend "the legend of the inquisitorial, ignorant, fanatical Spain, incapable of figuring among civilized nations today as well as in the past, always ready for violent repressions; enemy of progress and innovations."
2. "The Ninety-Five Theses on the Power and Efficacy of Indulgences" protested against clerical abuses, particularly the sale of indulgences (remissions of temporal punishment for sins which have already been forgiven), and other practices within the Catholic Church.
3. America is named after the Italian explorer Amerigo Vespucci (1454–1512), although he was not the first European to set foot on

the mainland. He is believed to be the first person, however, to realize that he had arrived at a separate continent and not the coast of Asia, as Columbus thought. The German cartographer Martin Waldseemüller is credited with the first recorded usage of America, in the 1507 map of *Universalis Cosmographia* in honor of Vespucci.

4. "La guerra civil, ¿cómo pudo ocurrir?" (1980), by Julián Marías, reprinted as chapter 12 of *Ser español* (Barcelona: Planeta, 2008), 255–256.

5. W. H. Auden, *Spain* (London: Faber and Faber, 1937). In the poem Auden called Spain "that fragment nipped off from hot Africa, soldered so crudely to inventive Europe."

Chapter 2

1. These figures come from the prologue to Paul Preston's book *The Spanish Holocaust: Inquisition and Extermination in Twentieth-Century Spain* (London: HarperPress, 2011).

2. Luiza Iordache, *Republicanos españoles en el Gulag (1939–56)* (Barcelona: Institut de Ciències i Socials, 2008).

3. "The political future of Spain," December 5, 1947, released under the CIA's historical review program.

4. Cited by the *New York Times*, October 28, 1951, which quoted a report by a US economic mission to Spain.

5. When Santiago Carrillo, the secretary-general of the Spanish Communist Party (1960–1982), was asked why a young person joined the party, despite all the Francoist propaganda against it, he said this was because the only way to be actively against the regime at that time was to be a Communist. Cited in *Dialogue on Spain* by Santiago Carrillo with Regis Debray and Max Gallo (London: Lawrence & Wishart, 1976).

6. Jorge Semprún (1923–2011) was too young to fight in the Civil War. He spent it in the Netherlands, where his diplomat father represented the Republic. During the Nazi occupation of France, Semprún joined the Resistance and was captured in 1943 and

deported to the Buchenwald concentration camp. He was expelled from the Spanish Communist Party in 1965.

7. Four people were killed in Lisbon on April 25, 1974, when the Portuguese dictatorship was overthrown in a military coup.

Chapter 5

1. These figures come from UNCTAD's annual World Investment Reports.

2. Henry Kamen, *The Disinherited: The Exiles Who Created Spanish Culture* (London: Allen Lane, 2007), xi (preface).

3. Report by the economic research office of Prime Minister José Luis Rodríguez Zapatero (November 2006).

4. José María Aznar, *Ocho años de gobierno: una visión personal de España* (Barcelona: Planeta, 2004).

5. *Retratos y perfiles* (Barcelona: Planeta, 2005), 265–274.

Chapter 6

1. Charles Powell, "Did Terrorism Sway Spain's Election?" (Philadelphia: Current History Magazine), November 2004, 380.

2. The first such commission was established in Chile in 1990.

3. The *Economist* magazine's house-price indicators in the issue of May 3, 2011.

4. The European Union defines early school leavers as people aged 18–24 who have only lower secondary education or less and are no longer in education or training. Spain's situation is not as bad as the statistics suggest; it sets a higher pass mark for the school-leaving exams than France, for example, whose early-school-leaving rate is half that of Spain's at 12 percent.

5. Figures calculated on the basis of the population and exports data in the 2012 World Development Indicators (World Bank).

6. Testimony by Luis Linde before the Parliamentary Committee on Economic Affairs and Competitiveness, July 17, 2012.

7. George Orwell, "In Front of Your Nose," *Tribune* newspaper, March 22, 1946.

8. Internal report by a Bank of Spain inspection team drawn up in March 2012 and cited in the newspaper *El País* on September 26, 2012.

9. Report presented by José María Fernández Norniella and cited in the newspaper *El País* on September 24, 2012.

10. This term was developed by James A. Robinson and Daron Acemoglu in their book *Why Nations Fail: The Origins of Power, Prosperity and Poverty* (New York: Crown Business, 2012).

Chapter 7

1. Eurostat, the EU's statistical agency, defines the Gini coefficient as the relationship of cumulative shares of the population arranged according to the level of equivalized disposable income, to the cumulative share of the equivalized total disposable income received by them.

2. See note 4 in chapter 6.

SELECTED SUGGESTED READINGS IN ENGLISH

Newspapers and news agencies

Euro Weekly News, based near Malaga on the Costa del Sol, is an English-language printed newspaper in Spain. It is free and has online editions (http://www.euroweeklynews.com/). The Olive Press is an English daily news website (http://www.theolivepress.es/). The Spanish newspaper *El País*, the leading daily, has an online edition in English (http://elpais.com/elpais/inenglish.html), and the Spanish news agency Efe carries some news in English (http://www.efe.com/efe/noticias/english/4).

Think tanks

The Madrid-based Elcano Royal Institute covers the main developments in the areas of foreign policy, the economy, companies, and other issues in an English-language report, published every month except in August, called *Inside Spain*, written by me (http://www.realinstitutoelcano.org—see the Inside Spain section). The publication is free and part of a newsletter, with some contents in English and others in Spanish. Elcano's website also contains occasional papers and analysis of Spain. FRIDE (http://www.fride.org/), also based in Madrid, monitors Spain's foreign policy every three months.

Books

Alonso, Gregorio and Diego Muro, eds. *The Politics and Memory of Democratic Transition: The Spanish Model*. New York: Routledge, 2011.

Barea, Arturo. *The Forging of a Rebel*. London: Granta, 2001 (first published in three volumes in the 1940s by Faber & Faber).

Barton, Simon. *A History of Spain*. London: Palgrave Macmillan, 2009.

Bates, Ralph. *The Olive Field*. London: The Hogarth Press, 1986 (first published in 1937 by Jonathan Cape).

Beevor, Antony. *The Battle for Spain: The Spanish Civil War, 1936–39*. London: Weidenfeld & Nicolson, 2006.

Black, Stanley. *Spain since 1939*. London: Palgrave Macmillan, 2010.

Brenan, Gerald. *The Spanish Labyrinth: An Account of the Social and Political Background of the Civil War*. Cambridge: Cambridge University Press, 1990 (first published in 1943).

Callahan, William J. *The Catholic Church in Spain, 1875–1998*. Washington, D.C.: The Catholic University of America Press, 2012.

Carr, Raymond. *Spain, 1808–1939*. Oxford: Oxford University Press, 1966.

———, ed. *Spain: A History*. Oxford: Oxford University Press, 2001.

Cazorla Sánchez, Antonio. *Fear and Progress: Ordinary Lives in Franco's Spain*. Oxford: Wiley-Blackwell, 2009.

Castro, Americo. *The Spaniards: An Introduction to Their History*. Berkeley: University of California Press, 1971.

Cercas, Javier. *The Anatomy of a Moment*. London: Bloomsbury, 2011.

Cervantes, Miguel de. *Don Quixote*. London: Vintage Classics, 2007. Translated by Edith Grossman.

Chislett, William. *The Internationalization of the Spanish Economy*. Madrid, Spain: Elcano Royal Institute, 2002. PDF available at http://www.williamchislett.com/public/InternationalisationSpanishEconomy.pdf.

———. *Spanish Direct Investment in Latin America: Opportunities and Challenges*. Madrid, Spain: Elcano Royal Institute, 2003. PDF available at http://www.williamchislett.com/public/SpanishDirect.pdf.

———. *The United States and Spain: In Search of Mutual Rediscovery*. Madrid, Madrid, Spain: Elcano Royal Institute, 2005. PDF available at http://www.williamchislett.com/public/ChislettEsp-EEUU-ingles.pdf.

————. *Spain: Going Places. Economic, Political and Social Progress, 1975–2008*. Madrid, Spain: Telefónica, 2008. PDF available at http://www.williamchislett.com/public/Spain_Going_Places_Chislett.pdf.

————, and Harry Debelius. *Coverage of Spain, 1975–78 for The Times of London*. http://www.williamchislett.com/transition-archive/.

Corkill, David, and Joseph Harrison. *Spain: A Modern European Economy*. Aldershot, UK: Ashgate, 2004.

Crow, John A. *Spain: The Root and the Flower*. Berkley: University of California Press, 1985.

De Blaye, Edouard. *Franco and the Politics of Spain*. London: Pelican Books, 1976.

De Madariaga, Salvador. *Spain*. London: Jonathan Cape, 1942.

Elliott, J. H. *Imperial Spain, 1469–1716*. London: Edward Arnold, 1963.

Encarnación, Omar G. *Spanish Politics*. Cambridge: Polity Press, 2008.

Esdaile, Charles. *Spain in the Liberal Age: From Constitution to Civil War, 1808–1939*. Oxford: Blackwell, 2000.

Fernández-Armesto, Felipe. *Columbus*. Oxford: Oxford University Press, 1991.

————. *The Spanish Armada: The Experience of War in 1588*. Oxford: Oxford University Press, 1988.

————, and Matthew Restall. *The Conquistadors: A Very Short Introduction*. Oxford: Oxford University Press, 2012.

Ford, Richard. *Handbook for Travellers in Spain*. Cambridge: Cambridge University Press, 2011 (first published in 1845).

Fraser, Ronald. *Blood of Spain: An Oral History of the Spanish Civil War*. London: Pimlico. 1994.

Gibson, Ian. *Fire in the Blood*. London: Faber & Faber and BBC Books, 1992.

————. *Federico García Lorca: A Life*. London: Faber & Faber, 1989.

Gilmour, David. *The Transformation of Spain: From Franco to the Constitutional Monarchy*. London: Quarter Books, 1985.

Graham, Helen. *The Spanish Civil War: A Very Short Introduction*. Oxford: Oxford University Press, 2005.

Graham, Robert. *Spain: Change of a Nation*. London: Michael Joseph, 1984.

Graves, Lucia. *A Woman Unknown: Voices from a Spanish Life*. London: Virago, 1999.

Guillén, Mauro. *The Rise of Spanish Multinationals*. Cambridge: Cambridge University Press, 2005.

Heywood, Paul. *The Government and Politics of Spain*. London: Macmillan, 1995.

Hooper, John. *The New Spaniards*. London: Penguin Books, 2006.

Jacobs, Michael. *Between Hopes and Memories: Spanish Journey*. London: Picador, 1996.

Jackson, Gabriel. *The Spanish Republic and the Civil War 1931–39*. Princeton, NJ: Princeton University Press, 1965.

———. *Juan Negrín: Spanish Republican War Leader*. Brighton, UK: Sussex University Press and the Cañada Blanch Centre for Contemporary Spanish Studies, 2010.

Kamen, Henry. *Spain's Road to Empire*. London: Allen Lane, 2002.

———. *The Disinherited: The Exiles Who Created Spanish Culture*. London: Allen Lane, 2007.

———. *Imagining Spain: Historical Myth & National Identity*. New Haven, CT: Yale University Press, 2008.

Kurlansky, Mark. *The Basque History of the World*. London: Jonathan Cape, 1999.

Labanyi, Jo. *Spanish Literature: A Very Short Introduction*. Oxford, UK: Oxford University Press, 2010.

Lannon, Frances. *The Spanish Civil War, 1936–39*. Oxford: Osprey, 2002.

Las Casas, Bartolomé de. *A Short Account of the Destruction of the Indies*. London: Penguin Classics, 1992 (first published in Spanish in 1552).

Marías, Julian. *Understanding Spain*. Michigan: University of Michigan Press, 1992.

Martí, José Luis, and Philip Pettit. *Civil Republicanism in Zapatero's Spain: A Political Philosophy in Public Life*. Princeton, NJ: Princeton University Press, 2010.

Matthews, James. *Reluctant Warriors: Republican Popular Army and Nationalist Army Conscripts in the Spanish Civil War, 1936–39*. Oxford: Oxford University Press, 2012.

Molinas, César. "A Theory of Spain's Political Class," *El País*, September 12, 2012, available at http://elpais.com/elpais/2012/09/12/inenglish/1347449744_053124.html.

Muñoz Molina, Antonio. "A Double Education." *The Hudson Review* 64, no. 1 (Spring 2011).

———. *The Depths of Time*. New York: Houghton Mifflin, 2013.

Nooteboom, Cees. *Roads to Santiago: Detours and Riddles in the Land and History of Spain*. London: Vintage, 1998.

Orwell, George. *Homage to Catalonia*. London: Penguin Classics, 2000 (first published in 1938 by Secker and Warburg).

Pérez-Díaz, Víctor. *Spain at the Crossroads*. Cambridge, MA: Harvard University Press, 1999.

Powell, Charles. *Juan Carlos of Spain: Self-made Monarch*. London: Palgrave Macmillan, 1996.

Preston, Paul. *The Triumph of Democracy in Spain*. London: Methuen, 1986.

———. *Franco*. London: HarperCollins, 1993.

———. *Juan Carlos: A People's King*. London: HarperCollins, 2004.

———. *The Spanish Civil War: Reaction, Revolution and Revenge*. London: Harper Perennial, 2006.

———. *The Spanish Holocaust: Inquisition and Extermination in Twentieth-Century Spain*. London: HarperPress, 2012.

Ruiz, Julius. *Franco's Justice: Repression in Madrid after the Spanish Civil War*. Oxford: Oxford University Press, 2005.

Serra, Narcis. *The Military Transition: Democratic Reform of the Armed Forces*. Cambridge: Cambridge University Press, 2010.

Thomas, Hugh. *The Spanish Civil War*. London: Penguin Books, 1977.

———. *Rivers of Gold: The Rise of the Spanish Empire, from Columbus to Magellan*. London: Weidenfeld & Nicolson, 2003.

———. *The Golden Age: The Spanish Empire of Charles V*. London: Allen Lane, 2010.

Townson, Nigel. *The Crisis of Democracy in Spain: Centrist Politics under the Second Republic, 1931–36*. Brighton, UK: Sussex University Press, 2000.

———, ed. *Spanish Transformed: The Late Franco Dictatorship, 1959–75*. Basingstoke, UK: Palgrave Macmillan, 2007.

Treglown, Jeremy. "A Heartless Craft: Spain's History Wars." *The Dublin Review* [Dublin, Ireland] 28 (Autumn 2007): 34–57.

———. "The Memory Movement: The Legacy of the Spanish Civil War." *Granta* [London] 105 (Spring 2009): 17–43.

———. "Franco's Friends." *Times Literary Supplement* [London], 30 March, 2012.

———. *Franco's Crypt: Spanish Culture and Memory since 1936*. New York: Farrar, Straus & Giroux, 2013.

Tremlett, Giles. *Catherine of Aragon: Henry's Spanish Queen*. London: Faber & Faber, 2010.

———. *The Ghosts of Spain: Travels Through a Country's Hidden Past*. London: Faber & Faber, 2012.

Trend, J. B. *The Civilization of Spain*. London: Oxford University Press, 1944.

Vincent, Mary. *Spain: 1833–2002 People and State*. Oxford: Oxford University Press, 2007.

Williams, Mark. *The Story of Spain*. Fuengirola, Spain: Lookout Publications, 2009.

Woodworth, Paddy. *Dirty War, Clean Hands: ETA, the GAL and Spanish Democracy*. Cork, Ireland: Cork University Press, 2001.

Wright, Alison. *The Spanish Economy, 1959–1976*. London: Macmillan, 1977.